Methuen

Methuen

AN ECLECTIC HISTORY

Dan Gagnon

Charleston   London

THE
History
PRESS

Published by The History Press
Charleston, SC 29403
www.historypress.net

Cover images: Top image is of Broadway looking north toward Central Square, about 1900. Bottom image is an 1842 engraving of central Methuen.

First published 2008

Manufactured in the United States

ISBN 978.1.59629.422.6

Library of Congress Cataloging-in-Publication Data
Gagnon, Dan.
Methuen : an eclectic history / Dan Gagnon.
p. cm.
ISBN 978-1-59629-422-6
1. Methuen (Mass.)--History--Anecdotes. 2. Methuen (Mass.)--Biography--Anecdotes. 3. Methuen (Mass.)--Buildings, structures, etc.--Anecdotes. 4. Methuen (Mass.)--Social life and customs--Anecdotes. 5. Community life--Massachusetts--Methuen--History--Anecdotes. I. Title.
F74.M6G34 2008
974.4'5--dc22
2008022618

This book is dedicated to my mother, Carol Connors Gagnon, and my father, Donald Gagnon, who encouraged and supported my history "addiction." I also dedicate it to my wife, Diane Gordon Gagnon, and my kids, Jeff and Katie, for putting up with my absences while I attended Historical Society and Historical Commission meetings, spent numerous hours pouring through the collection of the Methuen Historical Museum and looked at roll after roll of newspaper microfilm at the Nevins Memorial Library.

CONTENTS

CONTENTS

ACKNOWLEDGEMENTS

A work like this is not a simple task. It takes the assistance of many individuals to make it happen. I want to thank my Methuen history mentor, Ernest Mack, for sharing his love and knowledge of our city's past with me. My gratitude goes out to *MethuenLife* publisher Steve Whipple for providing me with a forum to present stories of Methuen's past to the public, so that they may appreciate the struggles and experiences of earlier Methuenites. I am especially indebted to the editing expertise of my National Park Service colleague Emily Prigot, who helped make my sometimes-crude attempts at writing into something that the public might want to read.

A special thank-you goes out to Mike Hughes, Lynn Smiledge and Stephen Barbin for their support and assistance in helping me prepare the stories for this book. Joe Bella and the late Red Winn were most helpful in allowing me to copy postcards from their collection for use in this book.

I am grateful for the help of library director Krista McLeod and her staff at the Nevins Memorial Library for finding obscure book titles located in libraries outside of the local network for me.

I wish to thank Marilyn Brough, Lionel Duhamel, Al Nault, Elisabeth Johnson, P.J. Watters, Randy Shipp, Winnie Medauer, Roger Gagnon, Don Maxey, Ken Doherty, Mona Hill, Robin Stolarz and Albert Retelle for taking the time to meet with me and share their stories. And finally, I want to thank Martha Briggs of the Merrimack Valley Preservation

ACKNOWLEDGEMENTS

Group, Inc., the members of the Methuen Historical Commission, Methuen Historical Society and Methuen Historic District Commission for their encouragement and support.

INTRODUCTION

*T*here have been few books written about the history of Methuen, Massachusetts. Those that have been published were written in a historical sketch style that only touched on interesting events in Methuen's past. This book is an attempt to tell, in more detail, some of those stories that I found to symbolize the spirit of the community. These stories are meant to show the influence world events had on Methuen and how Methuenites influenced the world. Many of the people portrayed in this book took part in world-shaping events, and in their own small way help determine the outcome.

Pulitzer Prize–winning historian David McCullough best summarized why it is important to tell these stories. He wrote in an article titled "Why History?":

> *The lessons of history are lessons of appreciation. Everything we have, all our great institutions, our laws, our music, art and poetry, our freedoms, everything is because somebody went before us and did the hard work, provided the creative energy, faced the storms, made the sacrifices, kept the faith.*
>
> *Indifference to history isn't just ignorant; it's a form of ingratitude. And the scale of our ignorance seems especially shameful in the face of our unprecedented good fortune.*
>
> *I'm convinced that history encourages, as nothing else does, a sense of proportion about life, gives us a sense of how brief is our time on earth and thus how valuable that time is.*

INTRODUCTION

To those Methuenites who helped get us to where we are today—thank you! For more information about Methuen history and sources for this book, please visit www.methuenhistory.org.

PART I

People of the Past

HERO OR SPY?

Methuen's most famous son, Robert Rogers of "Northwest Passage" fame, has been a source of pride in the community for many years. He is immortalized in the city's sports teams, and even the police force has his image on its shoulder patches. This farmer, war hero, author and playwright was also an enemy to our fledgling nation.

On November 7, 1731, Robert Rogers was born to James and Mary Rogers in a cabin near the corner of Cross Street and Hampshire Road in the northwest corner of Methuen. He was baptized one week later at the nearest church—First Church Congregational. He spent his first eight years in Methuen until his parents moved to New Hampshire.

Rogers was best known for his command of an irregular fighting force known as Rogers' Rangers during the French and Indian War. Rogers improved on long-used methods of fighting by developing his "Rogers' Rules of Ranging." This method of fighting became the basis of special military units today such as Special Forces, Navy SEALs and Marine Force Recon. Rogers once outwitted the enemies that were tracking him by putting his snowshoes on backwards to throw them off the trail. He was recognized as an outstanding leader and his service during the war helped with the defense of the colonies.

One of his most famous military expeditions was probably his most controversial. He led a raid on an Abenaki village thought to be the base from which the Abenakis and French attacked English settlements along the frontier. Rogers led nearly two hundred of his rangers deep into French territory toward the village of St. Francis. He expected to find hundreds of warriors, but instead found only women and children in the village. Though the rangers had explicit orders not to harm women and children, their anger rose when they saw scalps from English settlers hanging near the entrances of many of the dwellings. Rogers was unable to regain control of his men—many of the women and children fell victim to the fury of his men. Abenaki warriors got their revenge a short time later when they pursued Rogers and his men back to the English settlements. Though Rogers survived the ordeal, many of his men did not.

After the defeat of the French in 1760, General Jeffrey Amherst sent Rogers and his men to take possession of the former French forts on the Great Lakes. By 1765, Rogers was in London, England, and published *A Concise Account of North America*. At this time, he also published his journals of service in the French and Indian War. His service during Pontiac's War (1763–64) inspired him to write a play in 1766 about his opponent, called

Robert Rogers standardized irregular warfare, but spent almost as much time in the courtroom as he did on the battlefield.

Ponteach: or the Savages of America. This play is thought to be the first theatre production written in the New World.

Rogers eventually was given command of the northwest post of Michilimackinac, in what is now Michigan. From here in 1766, he sent out, on his own initiative, the first English expedition to explore the upper Mississippi and Great Lakes region. The goal was to discover the elusive Northwest Passage, but the expedition failed to even reach the Pacific as intended. Rogers's ambitions caused him to be tried for treason, but he was later acquitted.

During the American War of Independence, Rogers tried to get a commission in the Continental army, but General Washington felt Rogers's loyalties were with England. In fact, it was believed that Rogers was spying for the British. On the most important date in our nation's history, July 4, 1776, Robert Rogers was in Philadelphia, under armed guard for spying. He was able to make his escape and then joined the British army. He organized and commanded the Queen's Rangers, which saw service in operations around New York City.

One of the least-known stories of Rogers took place in September 1776. While recruiting for his new military unit, Rogers spotted Nathan Hale, a captain in the Continental army. Hale was in civilian clothes and scouting out the British army in the area. Rogers suspected that Hale was spying, but needed positive proof. On September 20, 1776, Rogers met Nathan Hale and pretended to be pro-American. He invited Hale to dinner the next day at his quarters to meet other like-minded men. Hale was hoping to set up a spy network with these men. A short time after Hale arrived at Rogers's quarters and told his story to those assembled, British soldiers surrounded the building and arrested Hale. The next day, Nathan Hale was executed in Manhattan for spying for the Continental army.

During this time, it appeared that the years had taken a toll on Rogers's leadership abilities. On the night of October 21, 1776, Rogers was attacked by a regiment of Continental soldiers who, according to one author's account, "inflicted upon his men a defeat so crushing that only the darkness and the defection of some of the American guards, prevented their annihilation."

Later, after he organized another unit of the King's Rangers, the command was given to his brother, James Rogers. A broken man, Robert Rogers returned to England, where he lived out his final years in obscurity.

Rogers died on May 18, 1795, "in poor lodgings, in a populous and busy part of south London." He left no will, and his estate, valued at £100, was assigned to a creditor. The final word on this son of Methuen and hero of the French and Indian War can be found in the archives of the British army. Robert Rogers's name shares the same page in England's pension records as the infamous traitor of the American Revolution, Benedict Arnold.

METHUEN'S PATRIOT OF COLOR

The traditional image of the Battles of Lexington, Concord and Bunker Hill are of Yankee farmers standing shoulder to shoulder against the might of the British army. For the most part, this is true, but a recent study by the National Park Service found that 119 of these patriots were of African or Native American ancestry. Methuen can lay claim to one of these men—a twenty-five-year-old man named Prince Johonnot.

Johonnot was born on July 6, 1749, in Boston. His first name, Prince, was a common slave name and indicates that he was probably born into slavery. By the time he came to Methuen, though, he had acquired his freedom and had some education.

In 1773, Johonnot married Mehitabel Emerson of Methuen and they eventually had at least six children. About the same time, the situation around Boston began to intensify. In reaction to colonists dumping tea into the harbor in protest of a tea tax, England replaced the civilian governor with a military general and brought in four thousand troops. Laws were passed that were designed to keep the colonists in check. Local government was abolished and British soldiers were sent to the surrounding communities to confiscate gunpowder and military supplies stockpiled there. As a result of this new threat, Methuen formed a minuteman company in 1774, under the command of Captain John Davis. Prince Johonnot was one of the first to join. Though the regular town militia drilled once a month for half a day, Johonnot wrote, "[Davis's] company was kept organized and drilled two half days in each week, when the weather would permit." The extra training prepared them for the growing threat.

As tensions continued to rise, the Methuen minutemen were officially enlisted with the provincial government on February 14, 1775. Their enlistment was for ninety days, with the hope that they would not be needed beyond that time. They didn't have long to wait.

In the early hours of April 19, 1775, word reached Methuen that the British regulars were out, marching toward the military stores in Concord. Johonnot, as a member of Davis's Company, marched toward Cambridge to cut off the British retreat. They were unsuccessful, but when they reached Cambridge, they did join with the forces laying siege to Boston. Johonnot and the Methuen minutemen were stationed in the Centre (Harvard) College building. When his enlistment ran out on May 14, 1775, Johonnot reenlisted, this time for eight months' service, as part of Captain Davis's Company, Colonel James Frye's Regiment. This force was part of a New England army expected to reach thirty thousand men.

"On the night of the 16th of June A.D. 1775," Johonnot wrote, "[we] marched to Bunker Hill, where a breastwork & fort were thrown up during the night and the next day [we were] in the Battle on that hill." Peter Brown, who fought at the redoubt with Johonnot, continued the description. "The enemy landed, fronted before us, and form'd themselves, in an oblong square in order to surround, which they did in part—after they were well form'd they advanced towards us in order to swallow us up, but they found a Choaky mouthful of us." He continued, " I was in the fort when the enemy came in, Jump'd over the wall and ran half a Mile, where balls flew like hail stones and Cannon roar'd like thunder, but tho I escap'd then it may be my turn next." Brown's description of the battle was one of the most vivid of those recorded.

Prince Johonnot survived this battle, though three others from Methuen did not. Nearly 1,600 men from both sides were killed or wounded in the conflict. Despite the apparent British victory, the authority of the English Crown still extended only as far as Boston Neck and Charlestown Neck. The Massachusetts Provincial Army controlled the countryside and continued to lay siege to the British army.

Three weeks after the battle, George Washington arrived at the headquarters of the Massachusetts Provincial Army to accept command. What he saw caused some concern. The New England custom of an integrated militia and minuteman units was one that was unacceptable in his native Virginia. Fear of armed slaves rising up against their master was a constant threat. For that reason, blacks, both free and enslaved, were not allowed in the military. To the shock of the 119 patriots of color who fought two major battles in the previous four months, Washington ordered that no blacks would be enlisted in his army. A stipulation was made that allowed those already in service to remain. It must have been in this climate, where blacks were not welcome, that Johonnot left the military service when his enlistment was up at the end of 1775. Johonnot's participation in the Battle of Bunker Hill was the last time the American army was truly integrated until the Korean War in the 1950s.

When Johonnot returned, he moved his family from Methuen to Goffstown, New Hampshire. A veteran of the war and a respected man, Johonnot was chosen as a surveyor of highways in Goffstown on March 2, 1789. It is believed that he was the only man in the study to have held a town office. He died in Goffstown on March 25, 1836.

For Johonnot and the other 118 patriots of color who fought in the earliest struggles for our nation's independence, the hope for equality was on the minds of each. The American Revolution and the contributions of these patriots of color awakened forces in our country that changed the relationships between Americans and gave hope to a future of equality.

THE WRECK OF THE SS *SAN FRANCISCO*

As twenty-year-old Edward Tenney sat in his cabin on the deck of the steamship *San Francisco*, his concern for his safety was growing. Hurricane-force winds were slamming into the ship and it was questionable whether the ship could hold together. Thoughts of his young fiancée back home in Salem, Massachusetts, must have flooded his mind as he prayed to see her once more. Little did he know that by the time the storm had passed, nearly three hundred passengers would be lost, Methuen native Edward Tenney among them.

Tenney was born in 1833 to John Tenney and his wife Mary Augusta Bartlett. He was the second of four children, and the only boy. Tragedy

Nathaniel Currier memorialized the disaster with this lithograph entitled, "The Wreck of Steam Ship San Francisco." *Courtesy of the author.*

struck the household of four-year-old Edward when his mother died suddenly. John was left to care for his four young children. At some time before 1845, John remarried, and by the time of his death in 1853, four more children were added to the household.

According to Methuen historian Ernest Mack, Edward's father was the town's first lawyer. He later became a justice of the peace and businessman. With all of this success, the Tenneys must have lived a fairly comfortable life in Methuen. The family home was located at what is now 30 River Street, which was surrounded by eight acres of land.

Edward's new stepmother, Augusta Elizabeth Sprague, came from a prominent family in Salem, Massachusetts, so it was not unusual for the Tenneys to travel to Salem to spend time with her family. It was during these trips that Edward met Lizzie Andrews. She was the niece of Edward's stepmother. Lizzie and Edward also had something in common—both had lost their mothers as young children. The Tenney and Andrews children were also close in age—Edward was the same age as Lizzie's older brother and Lizzie was the same age as Edward's younger sister. Throughout their childhood, they were treated as cousins.

According to Andrews family historian P.J. Watters, "When Lizzie turned fifteen Edward's eyes nearly bugged out of his head. He fell head over heels in love." From Harvard, where he was studying for a law

Left: Edward Tenney had this photo made for his fiancée Elizabeth while he was at Harvard. *Courtesy of the P.J. Waters Family Collection.*

Right: Elizabeth Andrews was secretly engaged to Edward Tenney. *Courtesy of the P.J. Waters Family Collection.*

degree, Edward wrote a whimsical letter to Lizzie, asking her to write back.

She did, and for the next three years Edward and Lizzie wrote to each other every chance they had. As their relationship grew, they tried to keep it a secret. Many times when Lizzie's cousin Joseph White Sprague returned home from Harvard for a visit, Edward would tag along. To the rest of the family, it appeared that he was just visiting cousins. In reality, he was courting Lizzie.

In the winter of 1853, Edward received word that his father was sick with tuberculosis. Edward left school to help with the family and to lend a hand with his father's business. Sadly, on April 8, 1853, Edward's father succumbed to the disease.

Edward wrote to Lizzie, "I have felt it a duty to give up my profession 'under existing circumstances.'" Edward was now the head of the household and felt that he needed to learn a more useful skill to support his family. He began "to study book-keeping, etc." in Boston.

In June 1853, Edward and Lizzie secretly became engaged. He was overjoyed with the prospect of marrying Lizzie and wrote, "When I reached home I felt like kissing everyone in the whole house. I was almost tipsy with delight." He still felt it was important to keep the engagement a secret. To Lizzie he confided, "I still think it would be unwise to announce it to the world." In time, Edward became restless in Methuen and wrote to Lizzie that he was "somewhat impatient to be in some business."

By the fall, Edward's uncle found a position for Edward. It was with the Alsop & Co. banking firm in Valparaiso, Chile. Edward must have received this news with mixed feelings. Alsop was one of the largest banking firms in the world. His success was almost guaranteed. But in order to succeed, Edward had to leave Lizzie behind.

In mid-December, Edward found himself in New York City, waiting for his ship, the SS *San Francisco*, to take him to South America and to his new job.

The *San Francisco* was a fairly new ship, with masts for sails and a steam plant to power the two huge paddle wheels located on the sides near the middle of the ship. It had been built only three years earlier. On this trip, the U.S. government had hired it to transport the Third U.S. Artillery to San Francisco, California. The main deck was rigged with a large structure that contained cabins, staterooms and officers' rooms. Equipment was stored below, along with many of the soldiers. Nearly seven hundred people were booked for this trip. This included the soldiers, their families and other passengers like Edward Tenney.

It had been raining for a few days, and Edward took the time to write a few last letters before the ship sailed. In all of them, he wrote about how much he loved her and how much he was going to miss her. In one letter, dated December 20, he pledged to Lizzie, "When I come back I hope to be better in every respect than I have been."

On December 21, the weather had cleared enough for the ship to set sail. One passenger wrote, "The noble ship glided through the waters as if she had known old ocean." This didn't last for long. Captain Watkins wrote in a report later, "On the night of the 23rd[…]we experienced a most terrific gale from the northwest, which continued to increase with great violence until it blew a perfect hurricane."

The situation began to worsen. At 3:30 a.m., the engines broke down, leaving the ship to the mercy of the seas. An hour and a half later, one of the masts was carried away, along with the sails and four of the lifeboats. At 7:00 a.m., true disaster struck.

A massive wave slammed into the ship near the large paddle wheels. The force of the wave smashed everything in its wake, scouring the deck clean and caving in a section of the deck behind the paddle wheels. The structure, located where the wave struck, disappeared in the water's fury, taking with it more than 150 people. Among them was Edward Tenney.

For eleven more days, the ship foundered at sea. Eventually, rescue ships appeared and saved those still on board the crippled *San Francisco*. Nothing was ever found of the others.

THOUGHTS OF HOME

Those who serve in times of war often are subjected to harsh living conditions and forced to witness things that even an insane person could not imagine. In times like these, thoughts of home and family take on even greater importance. To two families, the home at 176–178 Merrimack Street was at the center of their thoughts as they fought to defend our country in its first one hundred years.

James Fry had recently acquired some farmland near the Merrimack River, and by April of 1775, had almost finished building his house there. All that remained to do to protect the building from the elements was to finish the roof. But on April 19, an alarm was sounded for all members of Methuen's militia to assemble. British soldiers had left Boston to confiscate the military supplies stored on a farm just outside of Concord center and local militias were called to respond. The British regulars' move into the countryside was a threat to the safety of the colonists. James met the other thirty-one militiamen of his company near the home of their militia captain James Jones, and began the nearly thirty-mile walk toward Concord. Though they arrived too late to take part in the actual fighting, they waited just outside of Boston for the next three days until they felt that the British army would not attempt to come out again. Fry's Methuen home must have been on his mind as he waited for the British army to make its move. The building was exposed to the elements, and if a storm came before he could cover it, the interior might take some damage. Fortunately, after only a four-day absence, James Fry was allowed to return home with his militia company and finish his house.

Nearly eighty years after the famous Battles of Lexington and Concord, Leverett Bradley married a descendant of James Fry and moved into the old house on Merrimack Street. In that home, Leverett and his

The Fry-Bradley house (circa 1775) was located at what is now 176–178 Merrimack Street. *Courtesy of the Methuen Historical Collection.*

wife Catherine had at least five children. When the Southern states attempted to separate themselves from the rest of the country, Leverett recruited Methuenites to form Company B of the Fourteenth Regiment and became its captain. The regiment later became known as the First Regiment, Massachusetts Heavy Artillery. Among Company B's ranks was fourteen-year-old Leverett Bradley Jr. His younger brother Jerry, and a cousin George Brickett, soon joined him. Another cousin, George Frye, was a part of Company K.

During the nearly four years of war, the younger Leverett wrote home constantly. Early in the war, he wrote about the boredom of camp life, and time after time reassured his mother and sister that he was safe. For a person so young, his letters were wonderfully written, and gave the impression that he wanted to share his experiences with those whom he loved. Though he never admitted homesickness, he often requested things from home that made his life in camp a bit more homelike. On March 25, 1863, while stationed on Maryland Heights outside of Harpers Ferry, Virginia, young

Leverett wrote to his family, "I shall expect all the butter you can send, as we need it very much, having nothing to eat but our bread, coffee and beef. *I must have my butter!*"

In May of 1864, Leverett Jr. reenlisted and returned home on his first furlough in nearly three years. It was while on furlough that Leverett received word that his company had gone into battle and suffered heavy casualties. One can only imagine what Leverett felt when he heard that among the casualties was his cousin George Brickett, who was killed on the first assault at Harris Farm near Spotsylvania, Virginia.

As a newly promoted sergeant, Leverett Jr. returned to Virginia and took part in some of the heaviest fighting of the war. During the assault on Petersburg, Virginia, his brother Jerry later wrote, "I lost sight of Leverett soon after the engagement began, and of course was very anxious for his safety." When the battle was over, the sixteen-year-old Jerry Bradley went looking for his brother. He wrote, "no one can describe the feeling that was in my heart as I scanned the thin ranks of the regiment as they moved to the rear, looking for the one man above all others who was so dear to me, my brother Leverett. I soon made out the white shirt-sleeves. Although surrounded by the men of his company, I broke through the ranks and in a minute more were in each other's arms, hugging and kissing each other like a couple of sentimental school girls."

Though slightly wounded in the fight, Leverett made no mention of his wound to his family in his next letter home. Instead, he wrote about the capture of his other cousin, George Frye, and tried to reassure the family back home that the cousin was not in any danger.

By the end of the war Leverett had written to his family about every two weeks during the four years he was away.

Despite the years, to both Frye and Bradley, the concept of home was a powerful one. James Frye risked his life in 1775, defending the homes and families of those in the countryside. The very thought of losing his right to property was unacceptable. Leverett, on the other hand, looked upon his home as a sanctuary, where his loved ones supported him during a time of personal and national crisis. There is no house in Methuen that better symbolizes the various emotions of what a home can be than the simple structure at 176–178 Merrimack Street.

"Nothing but Extinct Craters and Barren Hills"

Within the walls of Methuen's Historical Museum can be found the artifacts, papers and photographs that document Methuen's past. One of the more outstanding items there is a remarkable fifty-year series of letters from a Methuen native about his life in late nineteenth-century Hawaii and early twentieth-century California.

Clarence Munroe Walton was born in Belmont, Massachusetts, and came to Methuen at a young age. His father Edmund had purchased a farm in the fertile valley area of town, near what is now 264 Merrimack Street.

Little is known about Clarence's early life, but farming must have had a defining influence. Throughout his life, farming in various forms had a role in all of his successes.

In late 1883, Clarence, twenty-seven years old, and his wife, Emma, left Methuen for Hawaii to start a new life. Letters written from Hawaii hinted that Clarence already had a job lined up as a carpenter. What led to this decision was not recorded, but the decision must not have been taken lightly. Hawaii, at the time of Clarence's travel, was a foreign country ruled by a king. Even the climate was foreign to those who were used to cold New England winters.

Their trip began in Boston and continued to Vermont, Montreal, Chicago, Ogden (Utah) and Denver before finally reaching San Francisco. At each stop, Clarence wrote to his family in Methuen about the places that they had seen. He often compared the lands that passed by the train windows to those he knew back home. He commented that he was amazed by the changes in the landscape when the train entered California. He described it as lush with vegetation. He was even more impressed with San Francisco cable cars. In one letter, he suggested to his father that Boston get them also.

On December 15, 1883, Clarence and Emma boarded the SS *Alameda* in San Francisco, bound for Honolulu. Clarence later wrote that they were surprised to discover that the captain was from Methuen. They referred to him as Captain Morse. It is not known if they knew his full name, as it is not recorded.

After nearly two weeks at sea, Clarence and Emma arrived in Honolulu. In their first letter to their family in Methuen, Clarence wrote that someone, who was referred to only as Summer, met them on the wharf. In later letters, it became clear that Summer was his boss and sponsor.

Clarence was impressed by Hawaii. He wrote, "After leaving the wharf everything changed as if we had stepped into a vast conservancy." Even the

Honolulu Harbor was a thriving port when this photo was taken in 1910. *Courtesy of the Library of Congress.*

local fruit was a novelty, though a novelty that he did not enjoy. He wrote, "Mango looks like a pear, but tastes like turpentine. What I have eaten I didn't think much of."

From this point on, Clarence and sometimes Emma wrote home about every two weeks. As a ship bound for San Francisco was ready to set sail, the Waltons had a letter ready to go with it. They described the islands (Oahu was "nothing but extinct craters and barren hills"), the temperature ("the glass shows 70–80") and their home (they shared the other half of Summer's house). In one letter, Clarence wrote, "Been here three days and seen the King twice."

This would not be the last time that they would be associated with the Hawaiian royal family. On a few occasions, Emma attended garden parties at the royal palace. Of course, she wrote of those experiences in detail. Eventually, Clarence was constructing stables for the king.

On one occasion, Emma wrote about witnessing the funeral of the queen's sister. She wrote, "In the procession were three Honolulu fire companies, the Hawaiian army—about 100 infantry and 20 cavalry and a rabble consisting of servants, state officers, etc." She observed, "Here the Royal people do not do their own wailing, but hire a gang of women to do it for them and it sounds rather comical to drive by in the street and hear the noise." In other letters, Clarence wrote of meeting other people from Methuen. There were quite a few hometown people living on the islands.

By the mid-1880s, there were rumors that the United States wanted to control Hawaii as a protectorate. Clarence was amused by the natives' response. He wrote to his father, "You talk of annexing the islands, some of the natives talk of annexing the United States to this Kingdom."

Though Clarence seemed to thrive in the tropical climate, Emma was not so fortunate. Letters constantly mentioned the poor health of

Emma. At one point, Emma left Hawaii for treatment in California for a stomach ulcer.

By 1888, Clarence was working on the Waihee Sugar Plantation on the island of Maui. He oversaw a gang of workers and constructed flumes, bridges and buildings. In a January 1888 letter to his father, Clarence wrote that his job as overseer and paymaster was a demanding one. He was forced to spend long periods of time away from home.

In August 1890, Clarence and Emma were blessed—Emma gave birth to a healthy baby boy, whom they named Monroe. Letters to Clarence's family in Methuen were now full of the stories typical of proud parents.

By the 1890s, the Hawaiian Agricultural Company was impressed with Clarence's management of the Waihee Plantation, one of its subsidiaries. It wanted him to manage the Pahala Sugar Plantation that it had just acquired. This plantation was the largest one owned by the Hawaiian Agricultural Company and was located on the south side of the island of Hawaii. In 1895, Clarence accepted. He was now responsible for the cultivation of nearly twenty thousand acres of land, which produced nearly 120 tons of sugar an hour. Clarence expanded the plantation's operations by introducing five hundred acres of sisal in 1898. The fibers from this plant were used to make rope.

For nearly eight years, Clarence's management of the plantation was successful. Production increased and the company prospered. He even found solutions to the labor shortage by accepting Japanese laborers. Clarence's salary reflected his influence in the company. A $350 a month paycheck allowed the family to live comfortably and also invest in the stock market.

While his professional life was on the rise, things at home were beginning to decline. In many of the letters to Methuen, Clarence wrote of Emma's declining health. His wealth allowed him to send his wife to California for treatment of an undisclosed lung disease. Despite his frequent upbeat reports, Emma never recovered; she died on December 18, 1895. He sadly reported the death in a short letter to his parents. He wrote, "I will write more soon for my heart is too sore now." According to a later letter, she died of a disease of the bronchial tubes.

As Clarence's job occupied much of his time, his son was sent to the home of a friend for care. About a year later, Clarence remarried and once again they could live as family.

Clarence made one decision as manager of his plantation that had devastating consequences for the business. He chose to plant a type of sugar cane that was best for the climate of his plantation but was also more susceptible to insect infestation. This decision was a gamble that proved disastrous. Around the turn of the century, insect infestation began taking its toll on the sugar cane. Managers in the home office were upset and blamed Clarence for the problem. Letters home reflected the frustration he felt. In 1903, the insect infestation was so bad that it left many of the fields barren, and Clarence felt compelled to resign from the company. His final letter from Hawaii described his disappointment at having to leave Hawaii and his optimistic plans for life in Southern California.

Though Clarence continued to write to his family about his later life as a successful California poultry farmer, it is the observations of this New England farmer living in nineteenth-century Hawaii that are so remarkable. These letters offer a glimpse of a world few at the time could ever experience. They also help us to appreciate that, despite the years and distance from Methuen, Clarence Walton and his family were never far from home.

"A MODEL OF PERFECTION"

The late nineteenth century was a time of prosperity in Methuen. The Industrial Revolution had taken hold and great wealth was available for those who were willing to take the risks. One man who accumulated unprecedented wealth during this time was the son of a grocery and hardware store owner named Charles Henry Tenney.

Charles was born in 1842 in Salem, New Hampshire, to John Ferguson Tenney and Hannah Woodbury. He was the youngest of four boys. Daniel

Woodbury was born in 1832, George Washington in 1835 and John Milton in 1839.

By the time Charles was eighteen years old, he and his family had moved to Methuen. Five years later, in 1865, he married Fannie A. Gleason of Methuen. They had one surviving child in 1867, son Daniel Gleason. The following year, Charles and Milton opened a hat factory called C.H. Tenney & Company on Broadway.

The hat factory was a successful business and operated for a number of years, but by the early 1880s, Charles was looking for new opportunities. He sold his interest in the factory to his brother Milton and went to New York to find his fortune as a hat commission merchant. At about the same time, Charles Tenney purchased the old Whittier farmhouse and some adjacent land on Pleasant Street. He planned to build a summer estate so his family could escape from the hot New York summers.

For the next ten years, Tenney improved the estate. He hired the noted landscape gardener Ernest Bowditch to work with him in designing the initial layout. The Gate House was remodeled and the entrance drive was created. The drive wended its way around the hill as it ascended, and the effect was an unfolding of the landscaped terrain as one approached the crest.

Near the top, in 1884, Tenney had constructed a stock stable to house his livestock. Like many wealthy individuals, Tenney had pedigreed cows, bulls, sheep and horses. He even raised deer on the estate. The stables were built to showcase not only the quality of the livestock, but also the success of the owner. The viewing area was elaborately decorated with ornamental woodwork made from antique oak. Attached was a dressing room for riders. The stables themselves were furnished with the finest details. To exercise and train his horses, Tenney later built a half-mile driving track on what is now the Tenney Grammar School property.

In 1890, Tenney began the construction of his mansion. A New York firm, Carrere and Hastings, designed a chateau-style building as the focal point of the estate and the design was published in *American Architect and Building News* that same year. The mansion took two years to complete, and by the time the Tenneys moved into the mansion in 1892, most of the grounds had been laid out and landscaped.

Like many wealthy families of the late nineteenth century, Charles also collected specimen plants. Similar to works of art collected in a gallery, Charles purchased examples of some very rare and exotic plants and had them incorporated into the plantings of the estate. Many of these nonnative plants have survived and have adapted to the New England climate. Their offspring can be found on the estate today.

Left: Charles H. Tenney built his mansion in Methuen so he and his family could spend summers with his brothers. *Courtesy of the Methuen Historical Collection.*

Below: The Gate House was remodeled by Tenney in the 1880s and was the summer home of Charles and his family until the mansion was completed in 1892. *Courtesy of the Methuen Historical Collection.*

Tenney was very proud of his estate and in 1896 joined the Massachusetts Horticultural Society. Each year, the society selected an estate upon which to bestow the prized Hunnewell Award. In 1899, the society visited Tenney's estate and encouraged him to submit the work for the award. In 1902, Grey Court was indeed selected as the winner and was described by the society as "a model of perfection." By that time, Tenney had constructed a teahouse, pergola and what was reportedly one of the first bowling greens in New England.

In 1904, Charles's wife Fannie died. Charles and his son continued to come to Methuen for the summers, but there were not many improvements or changes to the property after that. In 1919, Charles died. His son Daniel G. inherited the estate but rarely visited.

The property remained in the Tenney family until 1951. An agreement was reached with the town to acquire the estate, but before it could be finalized, Daniel died, and the town ran into some financial problems. Part of the property was given to the town for a school, now the Tenney Grammar School, and the rest was sold to the Basilian Order of the Melkite Rite for a religious seminary. In the 1950s, the mansion served as the seminary building, and in the early 1970s, it was used as a rehabilitation center for drug addicts. The mansion was burned in a series of fires in the 1970s, and what remains is an L-shaped arcade.

Today, Grey Court is still a magnificent place. The fully restored Gate House greets visitors at the entranceway to the drive. Behind the Gate House, the grounds have been restored to a level reminiscent of its heyday and the ruins have been stabilized to remind the visitor of what was and is now lost. Though one cannot witness the grandeur of the place during its prime, a stroll on the grounds can help to recall a time when a simple shopkeeper's son could accumulate great wealth and create an estate that would be the envy of all who saw it.

A Dream Fulfilled

It may be said that some of the most distinctive architectural landmarks found in Methuen today are the structures associated with Edward Searles. To some, the massive medieval walls near the center of town are reminders of a time when families of great wealth lived in our community. To others,

Italian immigrants built many of the walls along East Street. *Courtesy of the Methuen Historical Collection.*

they are physical evidence of their family's struggle to survive and of their opportunity for a new beginning.

In the mid-1890s, Giacobbi (Jacob) Pitocchelli, a young stonemason living in the Province of Caserta near Naples, Italy, heard that a millionaire in the United States, Edward F. Searles, was looking for stonemasons to construct buildings and walls on his estate in Methuen, Massachusetts. The area where Jacob lived was hit hard by an economic depression. Rising birthrates and decreasing death rates added to the problem. Jacob's home province was one of the poorest provinces in Italy, so the opportunity to find employment in the United States was a great blessing.

It was not in his plans to stay in Methuen. He left behind his wife and children. After each project was completed, he returned to Italy and to his family. These "birds of passage," as workers like him were called, expected that their stay would be brief. The language and customs he found here were very different from those in his home in Italy. Immigrants like Jacob were not particularly welcome and were looked down upon. The idea was to earn some money, then return home.

The work was hard and Searles was very particular in what he wanted. As the wall construction around his estate progressed, if a tree was in his path,

Searles had the workers build the wall around the tree. Today, evidence of this can be found along East Street, where notches in the walls indicate where trees once stood.

For nearly ten years, Jacob traveled between his home in Italy and the construction projects in Methuen. According to his family, each time he left for home he was asked to bring back more workers. Jacob traveled between Italy and Methuen fifteen times in the ten-year period, each time bringing back more workers. In 1906, shortly after his fourth child was born, Jacob made the most important decision of his life. He and his family would leave everything that they knew in Italy and make a new start in Methuen. The work appeared to be steady, so Jacob's financial situation was improving. Also, the growing Italian communities in Methuen and Lawrence would help the family assimilate to life in the United States. In fact, the Italian community in Methuen became so large that the area along Merrimack Street in the Pleasant Valley section of town became known as "Little Italy." Jacob and his wife Maria eventually had three more children in Methuen.

In 1936, Jacob passed away, after spending nearly forty years constructing buildings and walls for the town's wealthiest residents. The structures left behind are a legacy of the wealthy families of Methuen, but to the Pitocchelli family and to families of other Italian workers, they are solid evidence of their dream for a better life for their families fulfilled.

The Methuen Tragedy of Robert Frost

Robert Frost is arguably the most recognized, quoted and respected American poet of the twentieth century. In his lifetime, he published more than two dozen books and was recognized for his accomplishments by winning four Pulitzer Prizes. Though not much is written about his life in Methuen, his short time here had an influence on his later life and became the inspiration for some of his poetry.

Robert had a fascination with the written word. He studied the meanings of words and their patterns. Frost was able to pass on his interest to hundreds of students during his lifetime, but his first experience as a teacher was not a pleasant one. In 1892, Belle Frost, Robert's mother, had been given a class of eighth graders at the East School (site of the present Central School) in

Robert Frost lived in this home at 635 Prospect Street in 1900. *Courtesy of the Methuen Historical Collection.*

Methuen. A group of boys were repeating the eighth grade and were giving Mrs. Frost a hard time. Frost asked Reverend Charles Oliphant, the new chairman of the school board, if he could take over the teaching duties of his mother. Frost must have been very convincing, because Reverend Oliphant reluctantly agreed. It was rare that a seventeen-year-old with limited college training would be allowed to teach.

Robert believed a strong masculine hand was needed to handle these boys, so he purchased a supply of rattans for disciplining the students. Corporal punishment was still an accepted method of discipline and Frost was determined to take no nonsense from these students. Not long into the first day, Frost was forced to use the sticks when a student pulled a knife on him. Frost eventually earned the respect of the rest of his students, but when the term ended, he resigned to find other, less strenuous work. In a school board report for the annual meeting in 1893, the board wrote, "Mr. Frost, although young, bears an unusual record for scholarship and maturity of character and has shown marked address in the management and instruction of a difficult school." In later years, while living in Derry, New Hampshire, after Methuen, Frost needed a stable income while working on his poems. He fell back on his teaching experience and worked at nearby Pinkerton Academy.

In 1899, a doctor told Frost that his health problems were a result of his sedentary lifestyle. As a teacher, student, reporter and even as a mill hand, Robert's life did not involve a lot of activity. Frost had still not chosen an occupation for his life besides poetry, so when the doctor recommended farming as a good occupation, Frost was open to the idea. In the spring of 1899, while on a walk in the Methuen countryside, Robert met a veterinarian/farmer named Charlemagne Bricault. Frost had been admiring his farm and became convinced that chicken farming would be a profession that would be interesting and healthy for him. As a child in San Francisco, Frost had raised a few chicks in his backyard, so the thought was not new to him. Dr. Bricault offered to help him get started, and with the help of his grandfather, Robert was able to find a place to set up his farm at what is now 635 Prospect Street. With Dr. Bricault's help, Frost learned the basic principles of poultry farming and began raising chickens. Dr. Bricault helped Frost whenever he could by selling the eggs and chickens for him.

Everything seemed to be going well for the Frost family until the summer of 1900. Robert's three-year-old son Elliott had become sick during the summer. A local doctor looked at him and prescribed digestive pills. When Elliott did not get better, a trusted family doctor was called to look at the child.

Unfortunately, it was too late. When the doctor left, he told the Frosts that Elliott would not last the night. Robert and his wife Elinor stayed by Elliott's bed all night, but by about 4:00 a.m. Elliott had died. One can only imagine their grief, the unbearable pain of losing one's own child. Robert blamed himself for not calling the doctor earlier. Elinor went into a deep depression.

Historians believe that two subsequent poems came out of this experience. Both "Home Burial" and "Out, Out—" are about the death of a child. Frost once said that the first poem took him no more than two hours to complete and a family friend observed that the poem was too close to home. This experience found its way, in one form or another, in his later works. Historian Jay Parini believed that even fifty years after his son's death, on some level, Frost was still obsessed and found a way to use the pain in his works.

In the fall of 1900, Frost moved from Methuen and the place of so much sorrow to a farm in Derry, New Hampshire, where he wrote the poems that became his first two books.

Robert Frost enjoyed a long and interesting life, full of triumphs and tragedies. Though his time in Methuen was short, the events of his life here became important themes that would echo throughout his long and distinguished career.

"A LIFE OF KINDNESS AND CARING"

The Nevins family was one of three prominent, wealthy families associated with late nineteenth- and early twentieth-century Methuen. Their names appear on many community institutions. While most institutions honor the two generations of male leaders, one honors a woman—Harriet F. (Blackburn) Nevins. The Nevins Farm on Broadway in Methuen (owned by the Massachusetts Society for the Prevention of Cruelty to Animals) is a living memorial to her interest and commitment to the well-being of animals.

Harriet F. Blackburn was born in 1841 in Roxbury, Massachusetts, to George and Nancy Blackburn. Her father was an English-born machinist who came to the United States in the early 1800s. By 1861, he had accumulated some wealth in the textile industry and partnered with David Nevins Sr. to rebuild the recently destroyed Pemberton Mill in Lawrence.

Harriet must have met Nevins's oldest son during this time because in April 1862 eighteen-year-old Harriet married twenty-two-year-old David Nevins Jr. The couple lived in South Framingham and, according to Methuen historian Richard Fremmer, David and Harriet "had several children."

Unfortunately for the couple, none of the children survived to adulthood. It must have been devastating to the kindhearted and caring Harriet. The couple did find comfort in adopting a young girl named Elise and acting as guardians to a boy named Hiran Appleman, who later became a minister.

After Harriet Nevins's father-in-law died in 1881, she and her husband spent summers in the three-story brick home in Nantucket that they inherited from him. The Nantucket home was built in 1845 and was located near the settled area of town. In time, the couple looked for more privacy and for a home more suited to their increasing wealth. In 1894, they eventually built an elegant Colonial Revival, shingle-style home on the island for their summer retreat.

In contrast, Harriet Nevins's brother-in-law Henry and his wife spent their summers in the remodeled ancestral farm in Methuen. The farm building, which dated back to the late 1600s, was located where the Quinn Safety Building now stands. It is not recorded when Harriet became interested

The Nevins's ancestral home was located at Hampshire Street and Broadway. *Courtesy of the Methuen Historical Collection.*

in animals, but she would have been delighted with what she found when visiting her sister-in-law Julie at the Methuen farm. Fremmer wrote that "it looked like a zoo." He added, "The loud screeching of the foreign birds could be heard in the center of town. Horses and birds of all kinds would be seen on the landscaped grounds. Peacocks often crossed the Spicket River ending up as far away as Pelham Street."

By 1890, Harriet and her husband decided to move to Boston to live with his mother. Two years earlier, Eliza Nevins moved to suite 5 of the Tudor building on Beacon Street, leaving the Brighton estate she had shared with her husband David. For five years, Harriet and David Jr. took care of his mother, but in 1895, the seventy-eight-year-old Eliza died. Only three years later, Harriet's husband David Jr. also died, while on a trip to Europe.

At the age of fifty-seven, and widowed, Mrs. Nevins decided to move one last time. She must have had fond memories of her time in Methuen because shortly after her husband's death she moved to the ancestral farm from which Julie Nevins had moved after her husband Henry's death in 1892.

Harriet became active with the Massachusetts Society for the Prevention of Cruelty to Animals and eventually sat on the board of directors. Her love of animals could be seen in the many dogs and horses she kept. The Methuen farm was the perfect place at which to indulge her passion. The *Lawrence Evening Tribune* wrote, "The MSPCA found in her one of its greatest and outspoken benefactors." One of her donations was for an animal ambulance to transport sick or injured animals to Angell Memorial Hospital in Boston for care.

Nevins Farm was given by Harriet Nevins to the MSPCA as a gift in 1917. *Courtesy of the Methuen Historical Collection.*

Harriet's most newsworthy donation took place in 1917. She donated nearly 160 acres of land near her Methuen home to the MSPCA as a "rest and convalescent home for animals." According to the *Methuen Transcript,* "Mrs. Nevins [gave], in addition to the farm land and machinery, a generous gift of money [for] erecting the necessary buildings." The president of the MSPCA even moved to Methuen to oversee the operation of the new animal rest home.

Among the conveniences added for the animals were shelters and piped water stations, distributed about the fields for animals seeking shade or to quench a thirst. Street railway companies and even the Boston mounted police began sending their horses to the Methuen farm for rest. All Harriet had to do now to be near animals was to walk next door.

Harriet also took an interest in her employees. She had gardeners, house servants, a masseuse and a chauffeur. She provided a place for many of them to stay on the farm estate. She would come to know her driver John Kilmurray very well because she spent many hours being driven around. The *Lawrence Evening Tribune* wrote, "Almost daily she rode through the business district of the city accompanied by intimate women friends."

In December 1928, tragedy stuck Harriet's employee family when a drunk driver killed Kilmurray, who was delivering Christmas gifts to Harriet's friends when he was killed. This tragedy had a particularly hard effect on the aging Harriet Nevins. A friend believed that Kilmurray's accident actually hastened her decline. Nearly a year later, on November 14, 1929, the eighty-eight-year-old Harriet Nevins quietly passed away in her Methuen home, near the beloved animals she cared so much about.

Even in death, Harriet continued to show her kindness for those she held dear and her concern for those less fortunate. In her will, friends, relatives and loyal employees were remembered. John Kilmurray's family was provided for until his children became adults. Money was given to hospitals, libraries and to the rest farm she helped establish. The most unusual bequest was directed to the towns of Walpole and Methuen: erect "a fountain for the use of horses and dogs."

Harriet F. Blackburn Nevins's life was one of kindness and caring. She showed concern for those less fortunate, and compassion for the well-being of animals. The Nevins Farm is a fitting and tangible reminder of Mrs. Nevins's dedication and commitment to the animals she so loved.

UNTIRING DEVOTION

Before the United States entered the First World War, young men from Methuen were volunteering to help. In defiance of the president's call for neutrality, some went north to join the Canadian army. Others crossed the Atlantic to fight with the British. Merrill Gaunt found a less violent way to help. He joined a unique group of men who chose to serve, instead, by saving lives in France in the fledgling Motor-Ambulance Corps.

Merrill Stanton Gaunt was born in Rhode Island on July 12, 1891. He and his family came to Methuen when he was still young to establish a textile manufacturing business here. "Spud," as his friends knew him, attended Searles High School, but finished his last two years of high school at the Worcester Academy in preparation for college at Amherst. According to *The Amherst Memorial Volume*, published sometime after 1916, Gaunt played football and hockey but was known as a "sensitive and friendly soul...with a reserve which was sometimes difficult to penetrate."

During some summers at Amherst, he returned home to work in his brother's textile mill. This experience gave him an appreciation of the everyday challenges faced by the working class. *The Amherst Memorial Volume* suggested that this led to "an eagerness to investigate social conditions in this country." Later, as a seminary student at Harvard's Andover Theological

Merrill S. Gaunt was the adventurous son of Methuen textile manufacturers and died in France during the First World War. *Courtesy of the Methuen Historical Collection.*

Seminary, Gaunt joined the Socialist and Cosmopolitan clubs and even found time to work with boys' clubs in Roxbury, Watertown and Waltham.

Merrill Gaunt also had an adventurous side. After his sophomore year, Merrill joined the crew of a cattle steamer and later served as a second cook on a freighter bound for South America.

In 1916, Merrill found his greatest adventure in Europe. For nearly two years, a war had been raging in western France. Whole generations of young men were being destroyed in the meat grinder of war, and socially conscious students like Merrill were looking for ways to help. When a group of Harvard students heard about the great work being done by the Ambulance Corps on the front lines, they found their cause. These volunteers went to the killing fields of France to care for the wounded and retrieve the dead. For a sensitive man like Merrill, this was the perfect way to help.

In January 1916, shortly after midterm exams, Merrill and others from Harvard went to France as members of Section Five of Norton-Harjes Motor Ambulance Corps. Attached to the French army, their place of assignment was near the village of Verdun, France.

Merrill wrote, "It is a tremendous and merciless world here[…]War is neither brilliant nor welcome to those who stand the slaughter[…]I find myself in a mighty machine-like, and terrible world, with death a frequent

Veterans from as far back as the Civil War helped dedicate the square in the center of town to the memory of Merrill S. Gaunt on November 11, 1922. *Courtesy of the Methuen Historical Collection.*

and expected visitor[…]I invoke you to a serious life, not a gloomy one,—but a serious one,—a bloody earnestness,—for I hear the shells booming now, and I have seen their work."

As the battle near Verdun intensified, the work became exhausting. "I am now on twenty-four hour duty,—a day and a night running at the city and then back here, a little ways out, for a day and back again," wrote Gaunt. To a friend, he wrote, "To see men terribly mutilated and boys with their legs shot off and entrails out is to come here."

On March 27, Merrill began experiencing severe headaches, a stiff neck, fever and vomiting. He was taken to a hospital at nearby Bac le Duc. After doctors examined him, it was determined that he was suffering from a cerebrospinal meningitis. The disease attacks the lining of the brain and spinal cord, causing inflammation. Among those that survive the disease, many are left blind or deaf.

For nearly a week, Merrill hovered near death, but on April 3, 1916, the twenty-four-year-old theology student succumbed to the disease. His commander wrote, "He did his work magnificently and to the fullest satisfaction of his chiefs. He arrived at his post at a most strenuous time in the vicinity of Verdun, and by his untiring devotion undoubtedly contributed to the saving of many lives."

In death, Merrill Gaunt received many honors—France awarded him the Croix de Guerre; Worcester Academy donated an ambulance, naming it in his honor; and Andover Theological Seminary placed a tablet in his honor at the seminary. It was in Methuen where a more lasting memorial was dedicated. On Armistice Day, November 11, 1922, the Methuen Selectmen, along with the local post of the American Legion, dedicated Methuen's Central Square in his honor. The Merrill S. Gaunt Square serves as a reminder of the selfless actions of a Methuenite who wanted to preserve life in the midst of such destruction.

A Struggle for Basic Rights

On July 14, 1917, a procession of sixteen women holding banners walked in single file to the White House gates in Washington, D.C. They were protesting President Woodrow Wilson's lack of support for a basic right of democracy—a woman's right to vote. Each protester knew that she risked ridicule, physical abuse and even imprisonment for what she was about to do. For Methuen native Eleanor Calnan, it was worth the risk.

Eleanor was born in Connecticut in 1874, and came to Methuen about 1900 with her mother Julia after her father died. They lived in a house on Merrill Street while Eleanor supported her mother as a dressmaker.

In 1913, Julia died and Eleanor became the head of her household. The inequities of Eleanor's situation must have occurred to her. She had all of the responsibilities but none of the rights of her male counterparts. She felt she should have the right to influence political matters.

About this same time, the radical National Women's Party, headquartered in Washington, D.C., was starting to make headlines. The organization was working toward securing a woman's right to vote and believed that the political party in power should be held responsible for passing the necessary legislation. Eleanor became deeply involved and, by 1917, she was the party's congressional district chairman in Massachusetts.

As President Wilson's second term approached, the tactics of the National Women's Party changed. Members began picketing in front of

Suffragette Eleanor Calnan of Methuen was a leader in the Women's Rights Movement in Massachusetts and nationally. *Courtesy of the Library of Congress.*

the White House. No one had ever done this before for political reasons, so it received some notice. Women stood as "silent sentinels," carrying purple, white and gold flags and two banners. One banner said, "Mr. President, What Will You Do For Woman Suffrage?" The other said, "How Long Must Women Wait For Liberty?"

For months, women from thirty states came to Washington to take their turns in the protest. Many visitors to Washington looked at these protesters with curiosity, much like a carnival attraction. When the nation entered the war in Europe, attitudes changed. The protesters were now labeled as unpatriotic and even accused of aiding the enemy.

In June 1917, the government was fed up and arrested the first protesters. Two women were hauled into court on the trumped-up charge of obstructing traffic, but they were never brought to trial. Eleanor and the leaders of the National Women's Party clearly understood that opposition to the administration would not be tolerated. The women also realized that if the nation was fighting for democracy overseas, that same democracy should begin at home. Nearly half of the adult population in the United States was being denied its democratic rights.

For nearly two weeks, women continued to protest in front of the White House. Each time the women were arrested, then released. On

June 27, retaliations against these protesters intensified. Six women were arrested and given prison sentences. Though these protesters stood silently on the sidewalk, they were blamed for the large crowds that came to hurl insults at them.

Eleanor finally got her chance to protest on Bastille Day, July 14, 1917. She, along with fifteen others, carried banners with the French motto, "Liberty, Equality and Fraternity."

Doris Steven, a witness to the event, later wrote, "Their proud banner was scarcely at the gates when the leader was placed under arrest. Another took her place. She was taken. Another, and still another stepped into the breach and was arrested."

After a two-day trial, Eleanor and the other protesters were convicted again on the false charge of obstructing traffic. Each was sentenced to sixty days in the notorious Occoquan workhouse outside of Washington, D.C., in lieu of a twenty-five-dollar fine. Most were shocked at such a harsh sentence. The conditions at the prison were severe—inmates were not allowed to talk and the food was nearly unfit to eat. There was a tremendous public outcry, and after three days, the women were released.

This experience did little to dampen the spirits of Eleanor and her colleagues. In fact, it emboldened them. Protests continued, and the subsequent arrests were becoming a public embarrassment for the president. Wilson met with the leaders to try to explain that he had no control over the actions of Congress. He even promised that he would do what he could do, but the National Women's Party leaders didn't believe him. Woodrow Wilson had a reputation of being autocratic and the Democratic leadership of Congress would not act without Wilson's approval. Indeed, none was sent.

In September 1917, Eleanor was arrested again, along with others protesting at the White House. Each was sentenced to sixty days, but this time the prisoners would not be released early. When the leader of the National Women's Party, Alice Paul, was arrested a month later for her protest activities, the women decided to continue their protest in prison. They knew that they had broken no laws and were imprisoned for political reason. They began demanding to be treated as political prisoners and refused to do any work. Two of the leaders began a hunger strike. Others soon followed their leaders' example and began refusing food. Eleanor was among them. Reaction from the prison officials was swift. They had little tolerance for this behavior and began force-feeding the prisoners in a brutal manner.

Forty-one new protesters were brought into prison on November 15 and, during what later became known as the "Night of Terror," were systematically beaten and abused by prison officials. Word leaked out of the

Suffragettes frequently protested in front of the White House. This image shows protesters in February of 1914. *Courtesy of the Library of Congress.*

incident and the public began looking more closely at the National Women's Party and the issue of women's suffrage.

In November 1918, a Republican Congress was elected. Eleanor and her colleagues hoped that the new political leaders would deal more favorably with this cause. Unfortunately, the new Congress would not meet until December 1919, unless the president called it. Passage of the required legislation was now in the hands of the president. One vote was all that was needed to pass the law, and with the Republicans in office, they had their best chance.

Pressure intensified and in February 1919, Eleanor and fifteen of her colleagues were again arrested while protesting the president and his policies, this time as he arrived in Boston. These were the last arrests in the women's suffrage movement.

President Wilson called a special session of Congress in May 1919 to act on the amendment issue. A month later, it was passed. For the next year, the law made it through the state legislatures for ratification, and on August 26, 1920, the Nineteenth Amendment to the Constitution became law.

Methuen native Eleanor Calnan had endured hardships and sacrifices for more than two years in pursuit of the principles of our nation's founding. Though she received little recognition in her hometown, her dedication and commitment directly contributed to one of the most important pieces of legislation in our nation's history.

INVENTOR FRANK WARDWELL

On a warm summer day in 1891, Frank Wardwell found himself on the banks of the Spicket River with a fishing pole in his hand. The sun was beating down into his eyes, interfering with his favorite pastime. He thought that if he could make a device that he could put on his hat to shade his eyes from the sun, he and other sportsmen like him could enjoy their hobby hands-free. Frank Wardwell's solution, and his willingness to take the risks toward that solution, began a long and successful career as an inventor and entrepreneur.

Frank had spent a good portion of his early adult life at sea—first on a merchant ship and then later in the United States Navy. In 1869, he settled in Methuen. To earn his way, he found a job as a night watchman at the E.P. Morse Box shop. This job proved to be not very demanding. After working at sea with his hands for so long, Frank needed a more challenging job. He eventually found one at the Bowen and Emerson hat factory, where he learned the finisher's trade.

This was just the training he needed. For the next twenty-six years, Frank Wardwell worked in the hat-making industry, gaining experience that would help him in later life. He married in 1874 and started a family. He also involved himself in the community. As a veteran of the Civil War, he was a founder of Post 100 of the Grand Army of the Republic, a veterans' organization, and served as "officer of the day" for the organization. He was eventually the last surviving member.

In June 1895, while working at J.M. Tenney hat factory, Frank came to a decision. He had been working on the idea of a hat shade for nearly four years. On June 4, he had received a patent for his invention and by December, he had decided to quit the hat factory. He chose to take a chance and work for himself making the F.A. Wardwell's Adjustable Hat Shade.

The hat shade was a cotton device that looked somewhat like an umbrella with the center cut out. The outside was drab colored and the underside was dark green. It was designed to be placed over the hat to add more shade to the brim. The unique feature of the hat shade was that it could be folded up and placed into a case that measured seven and a half inches long by

These two advertisement photographs show Frank Wardwell demonstrating the use of his "Hat Shade." *Courtesy of Mimi Wardwell.*

one and a half inches wide, so that sportsmen could carry it in their pockets. This invention proved to be very popular.

Frank also invented a walking stick gun and applied for a patent. The patent was turned down because the invention was considered a concealed weapon and thus illegal.

Probably the most profitable invention Frank created was a loom picker. On May 23, 1899, he received a patent for this device. This invention was a component found on a loom that sent the shuttle back and forth to make cloth.

In 1899, the textile industry was still in full swing in the Merrimack Valley. The speed and accuracy of the shuttle flying on the loom was crucial to the efficient manufacturing of cloth. The loom picker Frank invented safeguarded the efficiency of the loom. Shortly after receiving the patent, Frank built a factory behind his home on Hampshire Street. His invention became a popular device for textile manufacturers in the area. Frank eventually hired other workers to help with the manufacturing. In 1916, he received another patent for an improvement to his original loom picker design and continued to manufacture loom pickers until his death in 1932. The company founded by Frank, Wardwell Picker Company, continued under his son's leadership, but by 1946, new technology was replacing the old. The son, Harry Pierson Wardwell, saw what was coming, so he closed the factory before it became a financial burden. With the closing of the factory, the active manufacturing of Frank Wardwell's inventions came to an end.

Frank Wardwell chose a path in life that few would choose. His inventive spirit led him to ways most would not consider. He took a simple inconvenience like sunlight in his eyes and turned it into a lifelong pursuit of inventions.

"The Story Has Gone Out"

In 1965, heavyweight boxer Muhammad Ali won the Edward J. Neil Jr. Award for boxing. By the end of his career, he earned the award another two times, an honor held by only two other boxers in the sport's more than sixty-year history. To those in the boxing community, it is understood that the award is given to the fighter who has had the most influence on boxing for that year. What is probably not widely known is that the award is named for a world-renowned sports writer and war correspondent who spent his childhood in Methuen.

Eddie, as his friends knew him, was born in Lawrence, Massachusetts, but moved with his family to 255 Broadway in Methuen at a fairly young age. He was educated in the local schools, including Searles High School and Phillips Academy in Andover. He eventually graduated from Bowdoin College in Maine.

After college, Eddie got a job with the Associated Press in Boston and shortly thereafter was transferred to Baltimore, Maryland. At the age of twenty-six, Eddie joined the sports department of the Associated Press in New York. It was there that he established his national reputation as a sports writer. For nine years, he covered many of the major sports events. Among his friends were such sports legends as boxing champ Jack Dempsey, boxing promoter Tex Rickard and baseball great Babe Ruth. In 1932, a story written by Neil about the Lake Placid Olympics was nominated for the Pulitzer Prize and won him an honorable mention.

Wishing to go where the action was, Neil requested a transfer in the fall of 1935 so that he could cover international events. He was sent to Ethiopia to cover the Italian invasion of that country. During the seven months he spent with the northern Italian army, Neil constantly found himself in harm's way and frequently crossed the line from witness to history to participant. On a bombing mission with the Italian army over enemy lines, the plane in which he was traveling crashed and he suffered a leg injury. During a riot in the Ethiopia city of Addis Ababa, Eddie ran a gauntlet of gunfire to bring Italian troops to the rescue of Americans trapped there. While in Africa, Neil wrote a column called "Typewriter Snapshots of the War." Before leaving Ethiopia, he received a medal from the Italian government.

In 1936, Palestinian Arabs rose up in a rebellion against the colonial British government because the colonial government had begun allowing increased Jewish settlement in Palestine. Neil covered the uprising by going on a raid with the Arabs. He was nearly captured by the British.

Shortly before he was sent to Spain to cover their civil war, Eddie was sent to England to write an article about the coronation of George VI.

In May of 1937, Eddie found himself in Spain with the Fascist insurgents led by General Francisco Franco. Frequently near the front line, Eddie once dashed within forty yards of the enemy to repair a cable station so he could send out a story. According to the *Lawrence Evening Tribune*, "as bullets struck a wall a few feet above his head he turned to a fellow writer [and said], 'The story has gone. If I'm going, I would rather go with the story on the wire than unwritten.'"

The memorial at the Neil playstead (ballpark) on Lawrence Street is dedicated to Edward J. Neil Jr. *Courtesy of the author.*

The war in Spain must have had an effect on him. In a letter to a friend shortly before Eddie's death, he wrote, "It's far more dangerous than in Ethiopia, for these babies shoot straight, and a large part of the time right at you." He also wrote, "I can tell you within a radius of 10 yards where a shell will land just by the pitch of the whistle."

On New Year's Eve in 1937, Eddie's career ended. Near the city of Teruel, Spain, he and three other reporters stopped in a square for lunch. They were heading to the front to cover the Battle of Teruel, which had recently begun. According to one account, it was bitterly cold and artillery shells whined overhead. Shortly before 1:00 p.m., the reporters returned to their car to warm up. They weren't in the car very long when a 75mm artillery shell exploded near the car. Another reporter wrote that when he reached the press car, he saw that the two sitting in the front seat were seriously injured. One of the two, a British reporter from *Newsweek*, was killed instantly. The other, from the Reuters News Agency, was unconscious and bleeding badly. Eddie was sitting in the back and was only slightly shielded by the others. The fourth reporter was only slightly injured.

Eddie was taken to a hospital with multiple shrapnel wounds and a broken leg. He was given blood transfusions and was operated on. More than thirty-four pieces of shrapnel were removed from his body. For a while, it looked like his condition was not serious and he would recover. He told a fellow reporter, "Tell my office I'm going to Paris as soon as I can and I will be all right again."

However, his condition was not all right. The wounds became infected and gangrene set in. On January 2, 1938, two weeks before his thirty-eighth birthday, world-renowned war correspondent Edward J. Neil Jr. died. The blue-eyed, prematurely white-haired former Methuen resident became the first American war correspondent killed in the Spanish civil war.

A baseball park on Lawrence Street now bears the name Edward J. Neil Jr. Children play in a park named for this man who contributed so much to our knowledge of sports and to our understanding of world events. Though he receives annual, national attention through a boxing award in his name, a local reminder of his roots is displayed on a bronze plaque in a field where generations of children participate in friendly competition.

A Woman Marine

In the late afternoon of December 7, 1941, nineteen-year-old Winifred McComish ("Winnie" to her friends) was just finishing Sunday dinner with her family in Methuen. A radio announcer reported that the Japanese had just attacked the military base at Pearl Harbor, Hawaii. Winnie and her family looked at the radio in stunned silence. Her father, a World War I veteran, knew this was the beginning of a costly world war. But the petite nineteen-year-old could never imagine that it was the opening act of a life-changing experience as a United States marine.

Winnie was the only child of Frank McComish, owner of an oil business in town, and his wife, Hilda. As a bright and popular student at Edward F. Searles High School, she was involved with the student council. While in the eighth grade, she met her sweetheart, Robert Medauer. They became inseparable, and as time went on, the idea of marriage became a possibility.

Winnie and Robert graduated with their class in June of 1941. Unfortunately, career possibilities for Winnie were somewhat limited. The country was still suffering under the effects of the Depression, and as a woman, many jobs were just not open to her. Winnie was fortunate; she found work in the local textile mills.

Marine Sergeant Winnifred Medauer, USMC Ret., was with the first group of Women Marines to arrive at Cherry Point Marine Corps Air Station in North Carolina. *Courtesy of Winnie Medauer.*

The attack at Pearl Harbor had sent shock waves throughout the country. Young men rushed down to the military recruitment offices to volunteer. The day after the attack, Robert went down to Boston to enlist with the Marine Corps. Unfortunately for him, the standards for the U.S. Marines were still very rigid and he was turned down because he had a slight overbite. He eventually found a place in the United States Army Air Corps as a radio operator.

Winnie began thinking about the role of women in the military. It took nearly six months for the military to recognize the value of having women in the armed forces. In May 1942, the army began accepting women, followed by the navy and eventually the Marine Corps.

There was reluctance in the military to accept women. The Marine Corps was particularly resistant to the idea. The U.S. Marines had a long tradition of accepting only men who met their rigid standards of physical condition. Arguably, they had a reputation of being the fiercest fighting unit in the world, and felt that accepting women into the ranks would tarnish that image.

The Guadalcanal campaign changed all of that. The Marine Corps received heavy casualties while taking the island from the Japanese. Because of this, and the expectation of future losses, Major General Commandant Thomas Holcomb recommended to the secretary of the navy that women be allowed to join the Marine Corps. The idea was that women could fill noncombat jobs in order to free up the male marines to fight.

Winnie joined the U.S. Marines in March of 1943. She had married Robert the previous year and began to think of how she could contribute to the war effort. After considering the Women Army Corps (WAC) and the Naval Women's Reserve (Women Accepted for Volunteer Emergency Serves, or WAVES), a photograph of a woman marine in uniform helped her decide that the Marine Corps was the branch of the service she would join.

The standards of acceptance for women marines were pretty straightforward. Winnie met all of the standards except one—a woman had to be at least five feet tall to join. Winnie was only four feet ten and a half inches tall. She was determined to join, and subjected herself to a stretching procedure to help her pass the height requirement. It didn't work, but a sympathetic doctor overlooked that requirement after hearing her story.

Boot camp took place at Hunter College in the Bronx. Winnie's class was the second class to go through training. Apartment buildings near the campus were taken over by the military and used as barracks. Winnie remembers her room was on the sixth floor. The elevator was not to be used by the recruits. She wrote in an unpublished memoir, "We straggled up six floors with all we owned." Part of the training was going up and down those stairs as they were told to get a book that the drill instructor insisted they have. Winnie wrote, "This went on with us crawling up the stairs on hands and knees[…]until all our books for the day's classes were with us."

Boot camp took six weeks and the training was similar to the training for men. The main difference was that the women were not trained to fight. Winnie said, "During that entire time I never touched a weapon."

After graduating from boot camp, Winnie was assigned to noncommissioned officer (NCO) school. She wanted to be a drill instructor. She felt that her childhood training as a dancer would come in handy. Eventually, she was assigned as a barracks NCO at Cherry Point Marine Air Station, North Carolina. According to Winnie, "we were logged in, '*the first women Marines on the base*.'"

This is where she discovered what other marines thought of women in the corps. According to Winnie, "in anticipation of our arrival [to the barracks], some of the men had taken all of the mattresses off the bunks, dragged them through the dirt out back, poured oil on some, urinated on others. They were absolutely filthy and covered with vermin. They had been brought back into the squad rooms and put back on the bunks." That wasn't all the destruction they found. The bathrooms had been trashed—toilets stuffed with paper and lockers were smeared with chocolate cake and were crawling with cockroaches.

Winnie admitted that at first she was overwhelmed. Eventually, she got mad! Other marines, men, were called in to clean up the place, and by the time the rest of the women marines arrived, everything was cleaned up.

Word of incidents like this reached the commandant of the Marine Corps and a directive was sent out placing the blame for this type of activity on the unit commanders. After that, there were very few similar incidents. Eventually, the male marines came to appreciate the benefits of women marines nearby—some for their companionship, but mostly for the contributions they were providing for the war effort.

In the winter of 1944, Winnie received a call from Fort Dix hospital. Her husband Robert had been seriously injured in an airplane accident. His legs had been caught in his parachute lines, so when he landed his left knee was broken and his right ankle was shattered. No one else on the plane was injured. Winnie was given emergency leave to be with him and eventually she asked for a transfer to the U.S. Marine base at Quantico, Virginia, to be near him. She got her transfer, but in typical military fashion, the transfer was to Chicago, Illinois.

For nearly nine months, Winnie served as the NCO in charge of the Aircraft Instrument School. The separation must have taken a toll. When, in April 1945, she was told that Robert was going to be discharged, Winnie was encouraged to request an early discharge. It was accepted, and she began her new role as wife and nurse to her recovering husband.

Winnie's experience in the military was not unique. About 300,000 women served in uniform during the Second World War. The Marine Corps alone accepted nearly 17,000 women. Their determination, commitment and contribution to the war effort helped break down gender barriers not only in the military but also in the workplace.

Chaos on Pork Chop Hill

In July of 1953, Methuen native Roger Gagnon was being sent to a place no sane person could wish to go—a hotly contested outpost called Pork Chop Hill. Roger had been in combat for nearly seven months, but what he would experience on the rocky, barren terrain of North Korea was something that would stay with him for a lifetime.

Roger Gagnon was drafted into the army in July 1952; in January 1953, he was sent to Korea. The Seventh Division had suffered heavy casualties during the previous months and Roger was one of the thousands of replacements needed to fill the ranks.

For nearly six months, Roger's unit was involved in combat patrols just west of a pork chop–shaped hill listed on maps as "Hill 255." Roger's unit was under attack almost daily.

On the evening of July 6, 1953, Communist Chinese army forces attacked an outpost on Hill 255. It became almost immediately evident that this was going to be a major push by the Chinese to take the hill. Three months earlier, the Chinese had attacked Pork Chop, but U.S. forces were able to keep them off. This time, the Chinese were more determined than ever to gain the high ground. It was a threat to their front line. Fighting was fierce and, at times, the Chinese overran American positions, cutting off communications with other units. It became increasingly difficult to determine the locations of friendly troops. For five days, more and more soldiers were sent into the fight as casualties increased.

During this time, Roger Gagnon was at the base of the hill on combat patrols nearby, waiting for his unit to be called to the front. In the early morning hours of July 10, the word came down that Roger's unit was going in.

For five days, Roger heard about the fierceness of the battle and saw the casualties coming back. He was under no illusion that this was going to be easy. In fact, at the time, Roger believed that he was not going to survive the battle.

Before dawn on July 10, Roger's unit, King Company, Thirty-second Infantry Regiment, began loading into armored personnel carriers to relieve others on the west side of the hill. The long ride up to the front must have seemed an eternity because they were under constant attack from enemy mortars.

By 9:45 a.m., Roger's unit arrived at the hill. They were immediately sent to the area they were to defend, replacing another unit that had suffered devastating casualties. An officer in Roger's unit, Lieutenant Don Maxey, described the scene: "It was near complete chaos in a maze of partially covered trenches on that totally denuded and pulverized hill." At times, enemy artillery was falling about three rounds a second.

The bunkers that were so carefully constructed after the April battle were now just a series of rubble, entombing American and Chinese soldiers alike. All that was left for protective cover were the connecting trenches covered with timbers. Space was so small inside the trenches that soldiers squatted, shoulder to shoulder, to stay out of danger. Roger found shelter in one of the trenches near his unit's assigned area. As artillery fell and enemy rifles fired nearby, taking their toll, Roger and the rest of his unit entered the battle.

At one point, as the soldiers crouched in the trench, a shot rang out and the soldier next to Roger slumped down, shot in the forehead. Roger thought that it couldn't have been a better-aimed shot and had to have come from nearby. Because of the crowded conditions, there was nowhere to move the dead soldier. Roger had to move the body to the ground and sit on it to look for the sniper. He saw him nearby and told his sergeant that he could get him with a hand grenade, but he was not going to count to three after pulling the pin. He had been taught that he should count to three so the grenade would explode when it landed. Roger had only a small opening through which he could throw the grenade. If he missed and the grenade came back, he still had time to pick it up and throw again. Roger threw the grenade and it landed at the feet of the enemy. Roger took another look and saw the grenade coming back at him—the Chinese soldier had picked it up and threw it back. Roger told everyone in the trench to duck and the grenade exploded. Fortunately for Roger and the others, the grenade exploded outside of the opening.

Steady fighting continued throughout the day, but at 3:30 a.m., the Chinese increased the pressure by attacking with a battalion-sized force.

Roger (right) and his twin brother, Armand, served in Korea at the same time. This 1953 photo is the only one showing both of them in the war. *Courtesy of Roger Gagnon.*

With nearly eight hundred men attacking the American positions, more defensive positions were lost.

A decision was eventually reached that to continue to hold onto fortifications "was fruitless in view of the expected toll of casualties and the complete loss of tactical value of Pork Chop." The Americans would evacuate.

At 12:35 p.m., Roger's unit was told of the evacuation. Armored personnel carriers would begin evacuating the wounded, then the dead and then the survivors. By evacuating in the armored personnel carriers, the Chinese would think that soldiers were being reinforced. The plan worked. By 7:20 p.m., Pork Chop Hill was abandoned and the Chinese remained unaware.

It took the Chinese some time to discover the ruse, but when they began occupying the areas the Americans had so strongly defended, they were met with one of the largest artillery attacks the Americans would unleash during the war. Roger said that the hill once had a series of bumps at the crest, but once the artillery was done, the hill was flat. The Chinese won their hill, but at great cost.

The Battle of Pork Chop Hill was a costly one. Nearly 1,200 American soldiers were either killed or wounded in this six-day battle. Roger was one of the lucky ones. He didn't come home with injuries or scars. Instead, he came home with an appreciation of life that only those who have witnessed the worst that man has to offer can understand. That is what will stay with him for a lifetime.

PART II

Connections to the Past

THE DAMMED SPICKET

The Spicket River snakes its way from a northern spot in New Hampshire, through Methuen and Lawrence and then empties into the Merrimack River. Near the center of town, the river drops nearly forty feet within a very short distance to form a waterfall. This became known as Spicket Falls. When early settlers placed their first dam just north of the falls to power a mill, little did they realize they would change the future of Methuen.

Early records show that as early as 1709, a sawmill was located near the falls. Water was diverted to the mill and powered a simple up-and-down saw. Virgin forests lined the banks of the river for miles, so business must have been booming. As forests were cleared for farms, the mill at the falls changed to meet a new demand. A gristmill replaced the sawmill.

In 1812, Haverhill lawyer Stephen Minot built the first cotton mill, probably a spinning mill on the Hampshire Street side of the falls, where cotton was spun into yarn for local weavers to make into cloth. Unfortunately, in 1818, the mill burned down and had to be replaced. In 1821, a group of investors purchased the mill and the water rights, and formed the Methuen Cotton Company, copying the successes of Lowell and Waltham. Five years later, a brick factory building was built on what is now Osgood Street, bringing the Industrial Revolution to Methuen.

This mill was an integrated factory, where all of the steps needed to make cloth were carried out in one building. Just a few years before, the Boston Manufacturing Company in Waltham found success using this method. Work, once done in the home by women, was now reduced to individual tasks. This allowed unskilled workers to do the job for less pay. The Methuen Cotton Company hired young women from the farms in the area, who welcomed the employment opportunity. Many factory owners tried recruiting women by depicting the factory life as similar to home life, but with more opportunities. The 1837 image of the Methuen Cotton Company showed the mill building with curtained windows, a horse and carriage passing idly by and young women in their Sunday best strolling the banks of the Spicket River. This image gave the impression that the factory was a pleasant place to work.

Unfortunately, the workers quickly realized that the factory was far from pleasant. In fact, a year after the factory opened, sixteen-year-old Abigail Mussey left her home in New Hampshire to live with her brother in Methuen. When she went to the mill to look for work, she was shocked at what she witnessed. "How I was filled with surprise at the sight presented to my view!" she would later write. "Thousands of spindles and wheels were revolving, the shuttles flying, looms clattering, and hundreds of girls

This granite-block dam on the Spicket River replaced a smaller dam in the 1880s when David Nevins quadrupled the size of the mills. This photo was taken about 1890. *Courtesy of the Methuen Historical Collection.*

overseeing the buzzing and rattling machinery! I thought I should never want to work in such a dangerous place as that." She even compared life in a factory to that of a prison. After a brief time as a weaver, Abigail quit. She was not the only one to think that factory life was not for her. About 1853, Edward Searles spent a short time working in the mill. His father Jesse had been an overseer until his death in 1844, and his uncle James presumably held a good position there also. Edward did not remain there long. He eventually quit to work for another uncle, Artemas W. Stearns, in his store in Lawrence.

Despite the unhealthy factory life, the company prospered, and Methuen with it. The population more than tripled in the first fifty years of the factory. During this time, a commercial district had formed just north of the mill, residential neighborhoods began forming nearby and other businesses started. The First Church Congregational, once the religious center of the community, also moved from the east end of town to near the mills. As final evidence of the influence of the mill, the first municipal building was built nearby in 1853.

With all of this growth and prosperity, you might say that the dammed Spicket, with its early mill, changed the course of Methuen history.

WALDO HOUSE

The building at 233 Lawrence Street is considered one of the finest examples of Federal-period architecture in Methuen. Towering nearby are two imposing granite columns topped with pure bronze tripods, accompanied by an equally impressive story. Although the mansion today is used as a funeral home, it is a reminder of the influence and success its nineteenth-century owners had in the community.

On April 6, 1825, George A. Waldo, a local businessman, purchased the property that is now 233 Lawrence Street from the estate of Bailey Davis. Mr. Davis had died a short time before and the estate was sold for $70.25. Waldo was born in Vermont and moved to Methuen about 1813. He had been referred to as an ambitious, clear-headed man. One newspaper account described him as "neat and tidy, but quite stern and decided in manner."

In 1823, George Waldo married Almira Bodwell and shortly after purchasing the property, he built his home. Not much is known about his early life, but the style of the house indicates that he was a successful businessman. In 1832, George was in the shoe business and two years later became the postmaster in Methuen. His success continued, and by 1845, he had built the Waldo block building on the corner of Broadway and Hampshire Street. At times, George served as town moderator, which indicates that he was respected in the community.

George died in 1850, and his family moved from Methuen sometime before 1860. By 1872, the property was sold to another local businessman, John Low. It appears that Low's life mirrored that of Waldo. Like Waldo, Low was in the shoe business, served as town moderator on occasion and was the postmaster in town for a number of years.

Sometime prior to 1888, John Low died and his widow Mary Low sold the property to a newly minted millionaire, Edward Searles. Searles had grown up nearby and was interested in purchasing properties surrounding his family home. Without immediate plans for the house, Mr. Searles gave Mary Low a lifetime lease.

Searles was constantly improving his property and this area was no exception. He made improvements to the house and laid out a small park along Lawrence Street toward Park Street. An October 12, 1888 *Methuen*

This photo, taken about 1905, shows many of the improvements Edward Searles made to the area. The improvements included the Searles High School, granite pillars and a stone wall. *Courtesy of the Methuen Historical Collection.*

The landscape of hedges and the design of the walls with a gate in the foreground indicate that Searles may have wanted this to serve as an entrance to his estate. *Courtesy of the Methuen Historical Collection.*

Transcript notice mentioned "two large stone pillars weighing twenty tons each, with head pieces, have arrived consigned to E. F. Searles." These are the granite columns on the property today.

The columns were made in 1838 for the Bank of America on Wall Street in New York. They were quarried from the same area in Quincy, Massachusetts, as the granite used to build the Bunker Hill Monument and Quincy Market in Boston.

It appears that Mr. Searles may have been planning to make this area the entrance to his estate. He built a low stone wall around the park and left a cutout on the Park Street side as an entrance for vehicles. The placement of the columns aligned with the opening and created a long driveway to the house, which would have served as a gatehouse.

Searles ran into a problem almost immediately. He didn't own all of the property he needed to make this happen. Prior to Park Street being created in the early 1800s, the Baptist Church owned the land abutting the Waldo property. The creation of the new street divided the church's property, leaving a small wedge of land on the east side of Park Street. The church refused to sell, so Searles had to abandon his plans. The Waldo house eventually became the home of the original Methuen Historical Society and, in 1960, the Pollard Funeral Home.

Today, this property shows evidence of its storied past. It serves as a reminder of those whose success and respect helped shape nineteenth-century Methuen, and with it the Methuen we know today.

The Stone Arched Bridge of London Meadow

On Hampshire Road, near the Salem (New Hampshire) line, a small section of an abandoned road lies between the highway and the street. As it spans the Spicket River, a stone double-arch bridge stands in danger of collapsing. Known today as the Sands Bridge, this example of nineteenth-century engineering is the last surviving physical link of its type to the area's past.

Before Methuen was first settled, it was discovered that this area, bordering on what is now Salem, New Hampshire, was good meadowland. Methuen historian Ernest Mack explained that the area was where many believed civilized land ended and the wilderness began. They called it

"Land's End Meadow." Over time, according to Mack, the name was corrupted to "London Meadow."

Methuen historian Joseph S. Howe recorded in 1876 that a tragic event associated with the area had occurred in February 1698. "Jonathan Haynes and Samuel Ladd with their two sons had been to London meadow from their homes, in West Haverhill, for hay, each with a team consisting of a pair of oxen and a horse. When returning home…they were suddenly set upon by a party of Indians." Hayes and Ladd were killed. The Indians "took one of the boys prisoner and kept him for many years; the other boy cut one of the horses loose, jumped on his back, and got away."

Thirty-one years later, the area was much tamer. About 1729, colonial soldier Robert Rogers's family came to this area of Methuen, along with others from Northern Ireland. According to Ernest Mack, James and Mary Rogers arrived with their four children and settled on land near the Spicket River, near London Meadow. The exact location of the cabin is not known because James never registered his land claim, but Ernest Mack determined that it was on land near what is now the corner of Cross Street and Hampshire Road. On November 7, 1731, Robert was born and was soon followed by two sisters and a brother.

The main thoroughfare in the area was a trail that connected Haverhill to Dracut and cut through Rogers land. Dracut Path, as it was called, followed mostly along what is now Hampshire Road, running toward what is now the Methuen Town Forest. According to Ernest Mack, the path "can still be followed over the hill through the Town Forest."

For nearly ten years, the Rogers family tried to make the Methuen farm successful, but in March 1739, the family moved north to what is now Dunbarton, New Hampshire.

Why the Rogers family left the fertile London Meadow area to settle the meadowlands of Dunbarton is unknown. What is known is that just three years before, in March 1736, a road was laid out from Methuen Village to Dracut Path. Perhaps an increased number of travelers disturbed the privacy of the Rogers family.

At the Spicket River, near their home, a simple plank bridge had been laid across for travelers. The harsh New England winters took their toll on the untreated lumber and regular maintenance was required. Every few years, the town records recorded payments to individuals for their work repairing the bridge.

By the 1830s, the town decided to replace many of the more vulnerable bridges with stone. Though the initial costs were higher than replacing them with wood, a stone bridge was more durable. It could endure the harsh winters and spring floods much better and over time reduce the costs of

The Sands Bridge is the last keystone-style bridge remaining in Methuen. *Courtesy of the Methuen Historical Collection.*

repair. Bridges near the center of town were replaced first, but in 1835, the town voted to replace the outlying London Bridge.

This new bridge was a stone arch–type of construction common in the eighteenth and nineteenth centuries before the introduction of steel and concrete. Solid abutment supports were constructed on each riverbank. A frame made out of wood was constructed over the river that followed the shape of the underside of the bridge. The stones were then set on the frame the same way a dry stone wall was built. No mortar was used to bind the stones together. Rubble and dirt were then placed over the bridge and the frame was removed. The strength of the bridge lies in the placement of the keystones at the top of the arch. If constructed correctly, the weight of the stones and rubble would compress on themselves and the abutments on the riverbank. A well-built stone-arch bridge could last indefinitely.

Unfortunately, London Bridge, later called Sands Bridge, was not a well-built bridge. Photographs taken in the late nineteenth century showed that the keystone on one of the arches had slipped. Despite this, the bridge continued to be used by horse, buggy and automobile well into the twentieth century.

In 1963, the construction of Route 93 had reached the New Hampshire border. Hampshire Road and the Spicket River near the Sands Bridge had to be rerouted to make way for the highway. As a result, that section of the river was cut off from the rest of the river and a new bridge was constructed near the other on Hampshire Road. The Sands Bridge was abandoned.

After nearly 130 years of use, the function of this structure changed. Although no longer needed for travelers to cross a river, it now acts as a bridge to the past.

WALNUT GROVE CEMETERY

Dr. Stephen Huse and other Methuen leaders met at the Baptist church on Lawrence Street on June 15, 1852, to discuss the creation of a new type of burying place in town. They envisioned a park-like private cemetery with trees, plantings and winding roads. It would be a reflective place where the living could go to escape the bustle of everyday life. Family plots would be established where generations of families could lie together in eternal rest.

After two years of planning, Walnut Grove became Methuen's first "garden" cemetery and came to represent a change in the way the community viewed the end of life.

As early as the town's founding, the challenge of where to place its dead was a concern. Town records showed that a burying place was to be laid out next to the new meetinghouse. But due to a dispute about the meetinghouse's location, the town went without a burying ground for a while. It is presumed that families either brought their loved ones to Haverhill or Andover for burial, or they established family plots on their farms.

According to Methuen historian Ernest Mack, "There was at least one ancient private burying-ground in town, nearly opposite the old Bradley House on (176–178) Merrimack Street." Also, according to Mack, "one version of the oldest town map list[ed] 'Whittier Burying Ground' on perhaps present day[…]179 Tyler Street."

Nearly two years passed until Methuen finally established its first burial ground. Town records showed, in 1728, "the subscribers have laid out a Grave yard southerly from the meetinghouse." The graveyard on "Daddy Frye Hill" on East Street became the town's first, and originally encompassed only one acre. In 1803, it was enlarged.

As the town grew, so did its need for additional burial spaces. At the annual town meeting in March of 1757, the need for another burying place was discussed, and committees were appointed to look at locations in both the west and east ends of town. Reports were submitted by June of that year but nothing was acted upon.

Walnut Grove Cemetery was the first garden cemetery in Methuen. Many of Methuen's prominent citizens are buried here. *Courtesy of the author.*

By 1772, it must have become apparent to town leaders that a new burial ground was essential. Richard Whittier came forward and donated one-quarter of an acre of land in the west end of town for a burial ground. Some believed that the land might have been part of a family graveyard because some stones dated to the early 1700s. Over time, that one-quarter acre grew to over thirty acres and became known as the Elmwood Cemetery on North Lowell Street.

Early in the nineteenth century, Methuen's industrial and commercial focus moved to the Spicket Falls area. With the population shift toward the center of town, many may have considered the Elmwood too far removed on the outskirts of town. In 1828, the town decided to create a new graveyard near the intersection of Lawrence and East Streets. This one-and-a-half-acre graveyard became known as the Village Burying Ground. For nearly three years, this graveyard lay empty, but in 1831, Colonel Osgood's wife died and was buried there, and others soon followed.

Originally, graveyards were not welcoming places. Simple stones were positioned near the location of the body, with no attempt at beautifying the graves or landscape.

Then, new ideas about graveyards and death began to emerge. According to a National Park Service report, "romantic perceptions of nature, art, national identity, and the melancholy theme of death" influenced the way graveyards were planned in the nineteenth century. Even our language was changing: "graveyards" became known as "cemeteries," a somewhat softer perception of the final resting places. People didn't "die," they "passed away" or "passed on." Even the craft of funeral management became more professional. The family no longer prepared the body for burial. An undertaker carried out the funeral preparation, and displaying the body for mourners became more common at funeral homes.

As a result, the design of cemeteries changed. Trees, plantings and sweeping views became an important part of cemetery design. Mount Auburn Cemetery in Cambridge, Massachusetts, was the first to use this design successfully.

In 1852, when Dr. Huse and the others met in the church vestry to plan the new cemetery, Mount Auburn was a well-known success. Land off of Grove Street was purchased from the Tenney and Wilson families and landscaping began. The layout was a radical change from the earlier burying places. Instead of straight rows with no walkways

---

WALNUT GROVE CEMETERY

A walk through Walnut Grove is like walking through a book of Methuen history. Many leaders and prominent citizens of the community are some of its permanent residents. Some of the names that can be found include Methuen historians Joseph S. Howe, Thomas Dorsey and the Reverend Charles Oliphant; Civil War veterans Albert Dame and Granville Foss; and industrialist Alfred Gaunt and his brother Merrill S. Gaunt, who died at Verdun during World War I.

The monuments tell the stories of Methuen's people. The Ingalls family lost four children in a twelve-year period. Most died before their third year and none reached the age of nine. Reuben Lawrence, a ship captain for an oil company, died unexpectedly in Kobe, Japan, in 1904. Frank Johnson was so proud of his military service that his stone has the carving of a Civil War kepi on top.

Of all the names found, the Tenneys are most prominent and probably most closely associated with Walnut Grove. George W. and Daniel W. Tenney each served as treasurer, and in 1906, Charles built a mausoleum near Railroad Street. In 1928, Charles's son Daniel G. Tenney built the Tenney Chapel in memory of his father. The building was constructed using recycled bricks and features stained-glass windows designed by the prominent artist John LaFarge. The ridge above the chapel is lined with monuments of Charles's brothers and their families.

between the graves, Walnut Grove was designed with winding roads that created pleasant views. Trees and other plantings were placed throughout the cemetery, adding a more tranquil landscaped atmosphere. Most importantly, the new cemetery was a welcoming, reflective space where the living could enjoy nature and think of those who came before.

Walnut Grove became the model for future cemeteries in Methuen. In time, Elmwood, in western Methuen, added the garden landscaping, and ethnic associations and churches created private cemeteries to care for and honor their members.

With the efforts of Dr. Huse and his colleagues, the design of the final resting place of loved ones was changed forever. It became a place where the living may be inspired by nature while honoring the contributions of those who came before.

FIREFIGHTING

In times of crisis, help is just a phone call away. In the case of the Methuen Fire Department, firefighters can be on the scene within minutes, ready to offer assistance. In earlier times, if a fire broke out, it took the help of neighbors with buckets to try to contain the fire. Often the building was a total loss.

The first reference to an organized fire department in Methuen wasn't until 1822. The newly formed Methuen Cotton Company was concerned about protecting its new investment of a cotton mill near the Spicket Falls. The company was reminded of the fire that had destroyed the original mill four years earlier. In 1822, the Methuen Company purchased a hand fire engine with the help of five other private citizens who shared half the cost. The fire engine was owned by the mill and stored on its property, but was made available to fight fires in the community.

A volunteer fire company operated the fire engine. Area residents would work their regular jobs, but if a call came in, they dropped what they were doing and went to fight the fire. Despite this, it was rare that a volunteer fire company could save a building once a fire started. Men would come from all directions to the fire, often arriving before the equipment. The best the fire companies could hope for was to save lives and contain the fire to where it started.

By 1846, the population of Methuen had grown tremendously. The center of town was becoming a collection of homes, shops and factories. In order to protect this area, the town voted to purchase its first firefighting equipment, a new hand engine they named "Spiggot." The Spiggot Fire Association, the first town-sponsored volunteer fire company, was organized to fight fires in the community. The town even constructed a firehouse on the south side of an island above Spicket Falls to store the equipment. Eleven years later, this fire company was tested with a major fire in the square. Though many buildings were destroyed, the fire company was able to prevent the fire from spreading.

Eventually, other volunteer fire companies were organized. Some operated at the same time, while others were replacements for obsolete equipment. They included the Tiger Engine Company, the E.A. Straw Steam Fire Engine Company, the Mystic Hose Company, the C.H. Tenney Hook and Ladder Company and the Paul Methuen Hose Company. As more and more equipment was purchased to serve the needs of a growing community, the 1846 firehouse became too small to store all of the equipment. In fact, the hose wagon was stored in the firehouse, while other equipment was stored in the basement of Town Hall at the corner of Broadway and Osgood Street. The horses were stabled at another location.

Because of the storage problem, in the fall of 1899, the town opened a new, much larger firehouse at the corner of Lowell and Railroad Streets. Charles Tenney donated a large fire alarm bell to the fire station as a Christmas present to the town. The cost of the land and building was $15,000. The town took out a loan for ten years to cover the costs. Each year, the town was required to pay only the interest on the loan and pay the principal on the tenth year. When the final payment was due, the town did not have the money, so millionaire Edward Searles made the final payment and donated an additional $51,000 to pay off other debts.

The Central Fire Station, as it came to be known, originally had three arched bays facing Lowell Street with decorative glass-paneled doors. The equipment was backed into the bays and the doors were hooked up to the alarm system. When the alarm went off, the doors opened automatically, allowing the horses to leave their stalls and position themselves in front of the fire equipment. The harness hitch was suspended from a quick-release rope and pulley. The horses could be in position and harnessed in a matter of moments. The horses got so used to this arrangement that as soon as the alarm rang they went into position. During the transition years when the fire department began using fire trucks instead of wagons, this became a problem. Fire Department historian Ken Doherty recorded a legend where one very intelligent horse "heard the alarm and bolted for the station. When

Only a few years after this photo was taken in the 1890s, this firehouse, located on Lowell Street above the falls, was torn down. *Courtesy of the Methuen Historical Collection.*

he arrived, he dutifully positioned himself in front of his old apparatus bay and waited to be hitched up." According to the story, the firefighters had to move the horse away from in front of their new fire truck so they could get to the fire.

In 1936, the Central Fire Station was enlarged to accommodate more equipment. Another bay was added to the east side of the building and a repair garage was added to the rear. As equipment became larger, there were other alterations to the station. Two arched bays facing Lowell Street and the entrance to Osgood Street had to be squared off in the 1980s to fit the newer equipment.

Today, the Methuen Fire Department has grown from its humble beginnings. Ninety-six men and women staff the four firehouses located throughout Methuen, answering over four thousand calls last year alone.

And unlike their predecessors, firefighters can be on the scene within minutes, ready to offer assistance. With this in mind, it is comforting to know that in times of crisis, help is just a phone call away.

A Fraternity of Odd Fellows

In polite company, it would be insulting to call someone an odd fellow. It implies that the person does not conform to society's rules. The person is different, not worthy of acceptance and a social outcast. To a group of people in Methuen, this label had the opposite meaning. It was a mark of distinction and acceptance. These people were members of Hope Lodge of the International Order of Odd Fellows.

The International Order of Odd Fellows has been around since the eighteenth century in England, and since 1806 in the United States. No one is really sure how the organization got its name, but some believe that it was because it was odd for common laborers to band together for fellowship and mutual help in eighteenth-century England. Others say it is because the original Odd Fellows came from various or odd trades, not from the individual trades found in the guilds. In any case, the name stuck.

In 1844, a group of Methuen men decided to create a local lodge of Odd Fellows. Though initially successful, Hope Lodge, as it was called, eventually began to struggle. Many of its members were sick and their needs strained its finances. By 1855, the lodge surrendered its charter. Fourteen years later, in 1869, a new interest in the organization emerged and a new charter was issued. By 1879, its membership had increased to 125.

The nineteenth century was a tumultuous time. The Industrial Revolution was in full swing here and though many people were crowded together in factories creating products for the market, there was a growing sense of isolation among these workers. In the past, if a person fell on hard times, the community would come together to help. As the population in Methuen grew, this banding of the community became less and less the norm. Mutual-benefit societies started forming. These organizations, such as the Masons, Knights of Pythias and the Odd Fellows, became places where men could join together in fellowship, be involved in community work and, most importantly, have access to benefits such as life and health insurance. For many, these organizations were the only places to get these benefits.

Another factor that drew people to these organizations was the belief that even an ordinary member, such as a person who worked at a somewhat-mundane job, could become a person of importance in the lodge.

The first meetings of the renewed lodge were held at Town Hall at 290 Broadway, but within ten years, the organization had grown so large that it had to move. New space was found on the third floor of a new addition to the Dodge building at 271 Broadway. Newspaper accounts of the time described the lodge quarters as being tastefully appointed with a cook room, banquet hall and two anterooms. The banquet hall was beautifully frescoed and housed an organ for entertaining. The *Methuen Transcript* wrote, "The place [was so] attractive to good men, that the noble principles of fraternity might be more widely diffused."

Over the next twenty years, the lodge prospered. Membership grew to more than two hundred by the 1890s. During this time, there had been talk of getting a more permanent home for the lodge. Opportunity presented itself in the beginning of 1898. A parcel of property on the north side of Hampshire Street was up for sale. An old shoe shop was

The Odd Fellows Building held Methuen's first post office. This photo was taken about 1905. *Courtesy of the Methuen Historical Collection.*

located on the site. For legal purposes, members of the lodge formed a separate association to purchase the land and build a structure. Local businessman Edwin J. Castle, who later bequeathed to the town money for cultural activities, was on the board of directors of this new association. The land was purchased, and in the fall of 1898, ground was broken for the new Odd Fellows building. Less than one year later, the new building was dedicated.

In keeping with the organization's prominence in the community, the new building became a local landmark. Its architectural design reflected the success of the organization. It was four stories in height and made of brick trimmed with limestone. Four massive stone columns stood near the main entrance. The first floor held the post office and two stores. The second floor was divided into seven offices and a small lodge room. The third floor had a large lodge room, and the top floor held a large banquet hall, with fifteen-foot-tall ceilings, a kitchen and a smoking room. According to the *Methuen Transcript*, the ceiling of the lodge room was steel, and the finish of the interior was "elaborate." When completed, this building was the tallest building in Methuen.

As a reflection of the times, the mid-twentieth century began an era of harder times for the organization. Shortly after the Second World War, interest in these types of organizations began to drop. Many of the things that attracted members in the past were no longer an advantage for joining. Work benefits and government programs replaced the need for the benefits provided by lodge membership. Fellowship alone was not enough. With fewer and fewer new members joining and a rapidly aging member base, it soon became evident that the organization could no longer sustain itself. By the late 1960s, Hope Lodge was an organization in name only.

Today, the only reminder of this once-thriving organization is the four-story building in Gaunt Square bearing its name. Hope Lodge of the International Order of Odd Fellows had played an active role in the community for many years. In its nearly one-hundred-year existence, it offered its members fellowship, acceptance and a shield against the stigma of accepting charity. The surviving building today stands as a symbol of its past prosperity and commitment to the community.

A Symbol of Tolerance

On Easter Sunday, April 18, 1897, the Augustinian Fathers from St. Mary's Church in Lawrence held a dedication Mass in the newly built church on the corner of Broadway and Park Street in Methuen. The church was named St. Monica, in honor of the mother of St. Augustine. This Mass ended a nearly fifty-year struggle to establish a permanent place of worship for the Irish Catholic community and ushered in an era of religious and cultural tolerance that is enjoyed in our community to this day.

In 1846, the Right Reverend John Bernard Fitzpatrick, bishop of Boston, purchased land on the east side of Broadway near the Spicket River in order to build a church for the growing Irish community in Methuen. Many had been driven from their homeland because of a horrific blight on the potato crop. Millions would eventually die from starvation and disease. Those lucky enough to reach the United States were looked upon with suspicion and fear. In fact, a nativist political party, the Know-Nothings, began to emerge about this time. Its fear was that the Roman Catholic Church, subservient to a foreign prince (the pope), was growing in power and could potentially exert political control over a large group of people. To counter the spread of Catholicism, the Know-Nothings attacked and burned a convent in Charlestown, Massachusetts, and tried to destroy St. Patrick's Church in Lowell. It was during this period that Right Reverend Fitzpatrick purchased the land for a church in Methuen.

To the Irish immigrants, the church was a sanctuary in every sense of the word. It reduced their sense of isolation and fear by feeding their need for spirituality and their desire to belong. It offered a place of familiarity where one could share cultural bonds with others. The church also provided schools that passed on their history, traditions, values and culture to succeeding generations. The church became the focus of the Irish community.

In Methuen, the first recorded Mass was celebrated at Town Hall on Christmas Day 1876. Until the new church was built, the town government permitted a weekly Mass to be celebrated in its government building. The generosity and goodwill of the townspeople and selectmen were never far from the minds of the parishioners.

By 1896, the foreign-born population was more than 20 percent of the community. Most of that population was Irish Catholic, and the demand for a church building increased. Architect Patrick W. Ford, an Irish immigrant himself, was commissioned by the Archdiocese of Boston to design a church for these worshipers. Ford was an accomplished architect

St. Monica Church was built by, and for, Irish immigrants in 1898, and was the first Roman Catholic church in Methuen. This photo shows the church shortly after it was built. *Courtesy of the Methuen Historical Collection.*

and had designed churches and schools for the archdiocese, many of which still stand today. It was believed he would be sensitive to the needs of Methuen's Irish community.

Late in 1896, the work began. With blueprints in hand, parishioners constructed the Gothic Revival church. It was completed by the spring of 1897 at a cost of $16,000. A permanent place of worship was now available.

Weddings, funerals, christenings and confirmations all took place on a regular basis. The church hosted a youth center and even sponsored a Boy Scout troop. This building became an important part of the community. It was even featured in magazine and newspaper articles as an important Methuen landmark.

By the 1990s, the parish had grown and the church building could no longer meet the needs of the parishioners. A new church building was constructed on the corner of Lawrence and Park Streets. The stained-glass windows were removed from the old building and installed in the new. The pews and altar were taken out and the building was left as an empty shell. In the early morning hours of August 10, 2000, the first Roman Catholic church in Methuen was torn down to make way for a chain retail store.

The 1896 St. Monica church building had become a symbol of the community's acceptance of people from various backgrounds and cultures. With its destruction, the memory of a time when Roman Catholics, and the Irish immigrant, were looked upon with fear and suspicion has been erased. In its absence, the lessons learned about a time of intolerance have been also lost.

THE TALK OF THE 1893 CHICAGO EXPOSITION

In early February 1900, pedestrians near the corner of Lawrence and Park Streets were greeted with an unusual sight. Standing on a lot of land near the cemetery was a large canvas-and-wood enclosure covering an equally massive structure. Millionaire Edward Searles, who was known to collect and display various works of art, owned the property. Speculation as to what was under the cover began almost immediately, but residents did not have to wait long. In the early morning hours of February 22, 1900, the enclosure was removed, revealing an impressive monument to the nation's first president, George Washington. This sculpture became the first piece of public art Edward Searles provided for the enjoyment of his community.

The sixty-foot-tall monument was made of bronze and marble. The white Cararra marble base was forty feet square and forty-five feet high, with ten-foot-tall bronze statues on each corner. The corner figures represented the four stages of our nation's founding—Oppression, Revolution, Victory and Cincinnatus. Between each figure was an eagle standing on a draped American flag. Midway up the base, above the statues, in special niches, were bronze busts of Washington's four Generals—Lafayette, Knox, Greene and Lincoln. At the top of the sculpture stood the fifteen-foot-tall bronze statue of a uniformed, standing George Washington. Inside the base, just below Washington's feet, a time capsule was placed with photographs of Searles and his wife, along with Joseph Howe's history of Methuen. By all accounts, the monument was an impressive sight.

Shortly after his wife's death, Searles began collecting works of art and placing them inside his estate on the corner of Lawrence and East Streets. The works of one artist in particular drew Searles's attention—those of American artist Thomas Ball. Ball, though born in nearby Charlestown,

The Washington Monument was unveiled to the public on February 22, 1900. It once stood in the park that the St. Monica School and Church now occupy. *Courtesy of the Methuen Historical Collection.*

Massachusetts, had moved to Florence, Italy, as a young adult to study sculpture. He quickly became recognized as a premiere American artist. His other works include the equestrian statue of George Washington located in the Boston Public Garden and the "Emancipation Group" located in Park Square, Boston, and Lincoln Park, Washington, D.C. Searles had Ball create minor works for his Methuen estate.

During one of his trips to Italy, Mr. Searles stopped at the studio of Thomas Ball and saw a clay model of a statue honoring George Washington. The City of Philadelphia had chosen Ball's design for a statue in honor of Washington, which they wanted to place in the city's Fairmont Park. By the time Searles visited the studio and saw the model, the City of Philadelphia had backed out of the deal, and Ball was left without a sponsor. According to some reports, Searles encouraged Ball to complete the work. It took ten years, and by the time of the 1893 Chicago Exposition, Ball was able to send the top portion of the monument to the fair. It created such an impression on the fairgoers that the sculpture won top honors.

After the fair, Searles purchased the complete monument and made arrangements to have it delivered to his home in Methuen. Searles had planned to make a private park near the front gate to his estate, and the monument was to be the focal piece.

This photo shows construction workers installing the Washington statue, placed on top of the monument in February 1900. *Courtesy of the Methuen Historical Collection.*

Once the monument was in place, Searles added to the park by installing two historical pieces. In front of the monument, he placed an early nineteenth-century mortar cast in Spain. Behind everything, he placed thirteen massive chain links that were thought to be from the Revolutionary War Great Chain that stretched across the Hudson River, near West Point, to block the British fleet from taking the fort.

The park became a local landmark, and for more than fifty years the community enjoyed this impressive work created by a famous artist.

In 1956, the heir to the Searles estate, B. Allen Rowland, decided to sell off Searles's Methuen properties. The park was offered to the town to build a primary school. Unfortunately, the monument, mortar and chain were not part of the deal. Mr. Rowland wanted to remove and keep them for himself. At the March 26, 1956 Methuen town meeting, voters discussed the offer. It was determined that the land was too small to meet the state requirements for a school. The voters thought that if they could convince Mr. Rowland to donate the land as a park, they would be interested in making an arrangement to acquire the monument also.

According to the town meeting notes, "It was voted to neither accept nor refuse the gift of land offered…but that the town ask Mr. Rowland for the privilege of discussing this with him."

Mr. Rowland gave a deadline of April 1 for a response to his offer of land. For some reason that has never been explained, the lawyer handling the request waited until April 5 to deliver the town's answer. By that time it was too late.

The property and monument were sold to the Archdiocese of Boston for the St. Monica School. In July 1958, the archdiocese sold the monument to Forest Lawn cemetery commissioners for their Hollywood Hills cemetery. By August, the monument was gone.

For more than fifty years, the monument stood as a reminder of our nation's founding. By placing the monument in public view, the community enjoyed a work of art from a premiere artist of the day. Sadly, through the negligence of a lawyer to respond in a timely manner to the request of a donor, the community has been deprived.

MERRIMACK PARK

In early May 1921, travelers along Lowell Boulevard in southwest Methuen began noticing construction along the banks of the Merrimack River. Many probably thought that new camps were being built for summer recreation. As the month progressed, a much more imposing structure began to take form. A massive roller coaster stood on the strip of land between the road and the river near the Methuen armory. This gravity-defying thrill ride was the beginning of Merrimack Park. For nearly fifteen years, Methuen's only amusement park served as an escape from the ordinary and as a place of fantasy and excitement.

For many years prior to Merrimack Park, trolley companies looked for ways to promote ridership on weekends. The companies were charged a flat rate for the electricity, so riders on weekends meant profits. For the price of a trolley ride, individuals could enjoy an afternoon in a country atmosphere, listen to music or just relax. According to amusement park historian Bob Goldsack, "The trolley parks were an instant success, bolstering revenues for the traction (trolley) companies while providing much appreciated recreation for the community."

Juniper Park at the end of Pelham Street, Maple Park off of Howe Street and Glen Forest near the Lawrence line were parks of this type. The most famous trolley park still operating in the area is Canobie Lake Park.

Merrimack Park opened to the public in May of 1921. This photo was taken shortly after the park opened. *Courtesy of the Philadelphia Toboggan Company.*

It was built in 1902 in nearby Salem, New Hampshire. Little is known about Juniper Park, and all that survives of Glen Forest are a few postcards showing a wooded area surrounding a stage.

In 1921, Merrimack Park was established. It is believed that the Eastern Massachusetts Street Railway Company built it, but no records survive supporting this. One thing was certain: it took a great deal of money to build. In the spring of 1921, portions of the land were cleared to make way for the attractions, and in early May, construction of the massive roller coaster began. The "Deep Dips, Out and Back" roller coaster ran nearly the length of the park and was the most prominent feature.

By the end of May, the park was ready to open. Saturday, May 28, 1921, was the day chosen, with a pre-opening dance held in the new ballroom the night before. One can only imagine the excitement as the first visitors entered the park. The bright lights, smell of popcorn and cacophony of sounds and music must have been overwhelming to the uninitiated.

According to local resident Al Nault, "The trolleys unloaded near the entrance and parked on two tracks about five hundred feet further down the road. After walking through the entrance you walked down a slight grade to the food stands under the roller coaster. The Midway was located down the center. On the river side there was a wharf with a boat for rides along the river." Historian Bob Goldsack also described the "Old Mill Chutes" ride, a whip, circle swing and "aeroplane" ride that swung out over the river. One of the features of the park was a carousel, built by the famous Philadelphia Toboggan Company, which also built the roller coaster.

Nault remembered going to the park frequently as a child because he lived only a short distance away. Local and big bands out of Boston played in the ballroom, and on special occasions, Al would travel by canoe with his parents to listen to the music.

Merrimack Park became a very popular place. Unfortunately, it occasionally also attracted a bad element. In August 1921, the *Methuen Transcript* reported that motorcycle officer Walter Nicholson was recovering from a beating he received from a group of young men at the park when he tried to arrest a man. Officer Nicholson received a broken shoulder, cuts and bruises, which kept him out of work for several weeks.

In time, other attractions were added. Dodgems, a kiddie coaster, a Ferris wheel and a penny arcade became popular for the younger set. A wooden swimming pool with a slide was also added, and on weekend evenings, the dance hall was the place to be and be seen. Weekend fireworks could be seen for miles around.

According to Al Nault, one of the more popular events at the park was the Labor Day Regatta. Canoes of all sizes raced along the Merrimack River near the park. Mr. Nault was particularly impressed with the twelve-man war canoes. This event was so popular that participants and spectators began arriving days before. Farmers across the river in Andover let these early birds camp in their fields. The campers would then cross the river to the park in their own canoes or be picked up by the park's boat and ferried across.

The Great Depression must have hurt attendance at the park, but Nault had some of his fondest memories of the park during this time. He said that the Murphy family owned the park then and lived in a house nearby.

In 1936, disaster struck. Just before the spring opening of the park, a devastating flood inundated the area. Unusually heavy rains, coupled with a rapid snowmelt in the White Mountains, caused the Merrimack River to rise nearly eighteen feet. All buildings and structures in the way were affected. Merrimack Park was no exception. Its location next to the river made it particularly susceptible to the vagaries of nature. A photo taken at the time showed the entire park under water. Most buildings were covered up to the roofline and many buildings were totally submerged. When the waters receded, the park was in ruins. The Murphy family salvaged what they could but the glory days of the park were gone forever.

THE FRENCH CHURCHES OF METHUEN

Jean Baptiste Michaud and his wife Armonia left the small Canadian town of St. Louis du Ha Ha, Quebec, for Methuen about 1897. With them were their eight children, ranging in age from toddler to young adult. Their goal was to make a living working in the nearby textile mills. They carried few possessions, having sold them to pay for their travel expenses. What they did carry with them few could see, but it would help sustain them through an uncertain future. Their prized possession was their faith in the Roman Catholic Church.

Jean Baptiste and Armonia were among the nearly 900,000 French Canadians to immigrate to the United States from 1840 to 1930. By 1930, nearly 337,000 were living in Massachusetts alone. Many were farmers in Canada escaping an economic depression. The mills of the Merrimack Valley offered hope.

Culture shock was what many French Canadians first experienced after coming here. Schools and church services were conducted in English and many only spoke French. Historian Gerard J. Brault wrote, "Cultural differences, the language barrier and rivalry among workers created[…]tensions." According to Brault, "many of the new arrivals began to stay away from church; nearly all felt uncomfortable in these new surroundings. They longed to participate in devotions conducted in French and according to their customs."

In 1872, French Canadian Marist priests formed St. Anne's church in Lawrence. Their purpose was to serve the French-speaking population in the area. Many of these immigrants living in Methuen attended Mass there.

Education proved to be a bigger problem. St. Anne's church was some distance from where many of Methuen's French Canadians lived. Brault observed that French Canadian schools were an important part of their life. He wrote, "The cornerstone on which the Franco-American school was built was the profound conviction that abandoning the French language was tantamount to abandoning the Catholic faith."

In 1875, Mrs. Louis Potvin solved that problem. She set up a school in her home on Pine Street near the center of town. For two years, Mrs. Potvin held classes there, but according to the church history, local opposition forced her to close. After a three-year absence, Mrs. Potvin reopened the school at 48 Lowell Street, and for the next thirty-three years, children were taught their faith and culture.

In 1912, a group received permission from the pastor of St. Anne's church to build a French Canadian chapel in Methuen. Property was purchased on the corner of Lowell and Union Streets, and a building was constructed. The first Mass of the Mount Carmel chapel was held on March 14, 1913.

The first floor of the box-like building had classrooms for the students and the second floor held the chapel. There were no permanent priests assigned to the chapel, so priests from St. Anne's church came each Sunday to conduct Mass.

In the fall of 1913, the school, named St. Joseph's, opened its doors to students. Two nuns from the Good Shepherd Sisters in Quebec came to Methuen to begin teaching at the new school, and about 160 students were enrolled that first year. Two lay teachers joined the nuns. The house adjacent to the school was renovated for the convent. Eventually, the house at 82 Union Street was purchased for use as the convent and the old convent became an annex of the school.

The 1920s saw an increase in both French Canadian population and church activity. Two distinct French Canadian districts began to emerge. One was located near the southwest part of town near the Glen Forest. The other was near the center of town, continuing northwestward along Pelham Street. Trolley lines serviced both places.

In 1923, the Glen Forest district followed Mount Carmel's lead by creating a chapel at the newly built St. Anne's orphanage at Glen Forest Park. That same year, Mount Carmel made plans to build a more substantial church next to the school building.

A large hill located behind the school and convent buildings had to be leveled to make room for the church. Beginning in October 1923, and continuing until the winter of 1924, church volunteers began removing the hill. About fifty-two people worked with trucks, plows and scoops. The work was made more difficult because of the rocky soil. Father Andre, who had been leading this church, decided to make something good out of misfortune. He had the stones put aside to use in the building of the church. According to parishioner Lionel Duhamel, "Farmers [also] brought stones every Sunday."

The foundation was laid in August 1924, and it took nearly two years to complete. On July 18, 1926, Mount Carmel parishioners celebrated their first Mass in the new church.

By the 1930s, the French Canadian presence in Methuen was quite substantial. It became apparent to the archdiocese that there needed to be some changes involving the Methuen chapels. In 1935, land was purchased

French Canadian parishioners built Mount Carmel Church with stones retrieved from their farms. *Courtesy of the Methuen Historical Collection.*

on Plymouth Street to build a church. It was named Ste. Therese de Lisieux, who was known as the Little Flower of Jesus. It was also decided that this new church and Mount Carmel were deserving of resident priests to minister to the parishioners' needs.

For more than sixty years, these two churches served Methuen's French Canadian community. With each generation, though, the link to their Canadian roots became weaker. English became the primary language of the French Canadian descendants, and the French Mass was eventually eliminated. By the end of the twentieth century, the Mass celebrated in these two churches was nearly indistinguishable from that of churches founded by other ethnic groups.

In July 2000, the last identifying link to its French Canadian character in Methuen was broken when the Marist priests withdrew from these churches. The Mount Carmel Church was closed completely and its parishioners moved on to other churches. St. Theresa's reorganized and combined with St. Augustine's of Lawrence under a new name—Our Lady of Good Counsel.

Through all of this, these descendants of French Canadian immigrants still carried with them the prized possession of their ancestors—their unbroken faith in the Catholic Church.

A Piece of the American Dream

The post–World War II years saw unprecedented growth in Methuen. Young men and women returning from the war were looking forward to starting families and owning a house of their own. New housing developments were cropping up throughout the community, but for many, the price was beyond their reach. In one development, inexpensive factory-built houses by Gunnison Homes answered the need.

The neighborhood around Oakside Avenue was developed in the early 1950s and was once part of Edward Searles's Oakside estate. It extended from East Street to the Lawrence line. A mix of house styles was built, and eventually twenty-four of the factory-built Gunnisons were assembled in the neighborhood.

Gunnison Homes was the brainchild of Foster Gunnison, a former custom lighting fixture designer. Gunnison had started a company to research and promote the manufacturing of houses using an assembly line process. Historian David A. Hounshell wrote that Gunnison "felt that the really important contributions (in architecture)[...]were those that involved mass production." He wanted to be the Henry Ford of house building. Gunnison's first company designed the MotoHome, which was the forerunner of the Winnebago-style motor home. He eventually left that company, and in 1936 started Gunnison Homes in New Albany, Indiana.

From the outside, little distinguished these houses as being out of the ordinary. Most are "capes" (Cape Cod style) or small ranches, usually built on a slab. One of the most distinguishing features of the exterior is the metal "chimney" on the roof. Some still have the steel casement windows of the original construction.

Each house was made of uniform-sized panels made of a waterproof, stressed, skinned plywood. The panels were standardized, with some having cutouts for windows and doors. The style of the house depended on the arrangement of the panels.

According to Gunnison historian Randy Shipp, "Each panel was constructed of wood studs and bracing members that were only $1\frac{1}{2}$ inch thick with $\frac{1}{4}$- inch plywood glued to each side." This made the wall thickness 2 inches. In comparison, houses constructed today have walls

This Gunnison house on Brewster Terrace is an example of the unique homes in the surrounding neighborhood. *Courtesy of the author.*

that are either 4 inches or 6 inches thick. Insulation was placed in the void space. Both interior walls and exterior walls were made of marine-rated plywood. Shipp recognized that the "result was a complete housing unit that could be shipped on a single trailer truck and assembled on the customer's foundation in a very short time."

The floor plan was very simple. The front door opened to the living room. A bedroom was next to the living room at the front of the house. Behind the front bedroom were another bedroom and a bathroom. Behind the living room were the kitchen and a utility room, which housed the heating unit. On the back wall of the utility room was the door to the backyard and a plaque identifying the individual identification number, model size and date that the house left the factory in New Albany, Indiana. Few of these plaques survive. More elaborate plans were based on this design.

Today it would be hard to find a Gunnison house in Methuen that hasn't been extensively remodeled. In many cases, additional rooms were added and windows replaced. Some have gone so far as to completely gut the interior and rebuild. Though the houses have changed over time, this Oakside Avenue neighborhood is a reminder of the postwar building boom and the low cost alternatives available for ordinary people seeking a piece of the American Dream.

List of Gunnison Homes in Methuen:

10 Arlington Street
26 Birchwood Road
30 Birchwood Road
34 Birchwood Road
6 Brewster Terrace
7 Brewster Terrace
11 Brewster Terrace
15 Brewster Terrace
15 Elmwood Road
19 Elmwood Road
29 Elmwood Road
33 Elmwood Road
36 Elmwood Road
43 Elmwood Road
44 Elmwood Road
48 Elmwood Road

49 Elmwood Road
56 Elmwood Road
97 Elmwood Road
55 Kenwood Road
63 Kenwood Road
93 Kenwood Road
88 Larchwood Road
36 Oakside Avenue
74 Oakside Avenue
78 Oakside Avenue
82 Oakside Avenue
83 Oakside Avenue
86 Oakside Avenue
87 Oakside Avenue
95 Oakside Avenue

THE METHUEN SKI HILL

The first snow, for many, creates an urgent need to hit the slopes and go skiing. For many years, Methuenites had to travel miles away to find a ski hill with a tow to get them to the top of a hill. In the late 1940s, Methuen opened its first and only ski hill in the west end of town near what is now the town forest. The owners—attorney Harold Morley, Les Martin and Chip Sheehan—named the place the Methuen Ski Hill. It had two hills, known only as the "Little Hill" and the "Big Hill." To bring skiers to the top, there was a T-bar on the left side of the Big Hill and a rope tow for the Little Hill. A one-story lodge was used for rentals and for warming the skiers.

This two-hundred-foot slope was ideal for both beginners and experienced skiers. It was no accident that this hill was selected. In the 1930s and early 1940s, west-enders of Methuen used the hill to ski. According to Methuen native Don Gagnon, the hill was only a fire path. "You took risks skiing on the hill, with all the trees and such a narrow path." By the late 1940s, the trees were cleared and it is presumed that a rope tow was the first lift to get skiers to the top.

In 1965, Albert Retelle and his wife Evelyn, along with three others, started a ski school there. In addition to the Retelles, Joanne Thwaite Raitt, Skeets Scanlon and John Weir were also ski instructors. According to Al Retelle, the school was a concession, separate from the business of the ski hill proper. They conducted a popular morning class for housewives and after-school programs.

The one-story lodge was enlarged in 1972 to a two-story chalet-style building. A restaurant was located on the top floor and the rental office and warming lodge were located on the first.

In 1973, the Retelles purchased the ski hill and ran it for seven years. They changed the name to the Merrimack Valley Ski Area and eventually expanded the programs to include seven different classes for all ages, from tots to adults. In fact, Methuen High School Ski team coach Mike Girardi learned to ski there in the after-school program. In addition to regular skiing and classes, the Merrimack Valley Ski Area hosted many races and tournaments. A 1978–79 brochure lists the facility as having three slopes (from beginner to expert), two Mueller T-bars, one rope tow, snow making,

For many years, Methuenites learned to ski at the Methuen Ski Hill. *Courtesy of Albert Retelle.*

Onetime owner of the Methuen Ski Hill, Albert Retelle, clowns around in front of the ski lodge. *Courtesy of Albert Retelle.*

machine-groomed slopes, a Ski School directed by PSIA director with twenty trained instructors, ski rentals, the National Ski Patrol, nighttime skiing with good lighting, a snack bar with warming lodge and the Buddy Werner Ski Team (ages five through fifteen).

Some of the more popular events to take place included high school ski team races, the town of Methuen Winter Carnival (sponsored by the Retelle family and the town's recreation department) and the Al Retelle Challenge. This last event started as a dare and became more popular each year. Contestants had to hike up the two-hundred-foot face of the hill carrying their ski equipment. At the top, they had to buckle on the skis (no quick-set bindings at that time) and ski down the hill. The first one down won. Al was often kidded about whether he could finish the race because of his "age." He was in his forties—hardly an old man.

Sometime between 1975 and 1977, the restaurant portion of the building was partially burned, but according to Al Retelle, "the building was so well constructed the first floor could still be used for the rental office."

During the blizzard of '78, in the height of the storm (when a state of emergency was declared), the ski hill was opened by 1:00 p.m. on the second day of the storm. Skiers couldn't ask for better ski conditions.

In 1979, the Retelles decided to sell the ski hill. It had never been a moneymaker. Rising insurance costs, uncertain seasons and changes to regulations governing ski facilities made it difficult to continue. The Town of Methuen was able to secure a recreation grant from the state to purchase the hill. By the winter of 1980, the town ran the area. After a couple of years of poor snow conditions, and due to the town's inability to find a concessionaire to run the place, the ski hill was closed down. A fire in the ski lodge in the late 1980s ended all discussion of reopening.

PART III

Events that Shape a Community

METHUEN IN THE REVOLUTION

In the early morning hours of April 19, 1775, a rider galloped up to the home of John Davis, a captain in Methuen's militia, and urgently beat on the door. When Captain Davis answered, he was told that the British regulars were out of Boston and on their way to Lexington, Massachusetts. It was believed the soldiers were on their way to arrest the leaders of a protest movement that spoke out against growing tyranny in the colonies. Men from Methuen, numbering 156 strong, responded to the threat. They chose to risk not only their lives, but also their family's well-being, to protect the basic rights we take for granted.

The Methuen minutemen didn't make it to Lexington in time to take part in the battle. On the way, they were diverted to Cambridge to protect the headquarters of the new Massachusetts Provincial Army. Once it was determined that the British regulars were not going to attack, many of those from Methuen returned home. Captain John Davis's company remained and became part of Colonel Frye's regiment, which was trying to starve the regulars out of Boston.

Nearly two months went by when Frye's regiment was ordered to Bunker Hill in Charlestown to build a fortification. Approximately 1,200 men, 47 of them from Methuen, arrived at midnight and began building the fort—not on Bunker Hill, but on the next hill closer to Boston, Breed's Hill.

When the battle took place the next day on June 17, 1775, Captain Davis's company was in the thick of the fighting. His company was one of the last to leave the fort. According to a Methuen historian, Joseph Howe, Private James Ordway of Methuen described the final attack of the British on the fort. "He said that when the ammunition ran out at the close of the battle, he laid down his gun and threw stones at the British until driven out." According to another account, as a British soldier tried to take Davis prisoner near the end of the battle, Davis ran him through with his sword and made his escape. That same account also said that as he escaped, "he took one of his wounded men on his back out of reach of danger." As he was crossing a hollow between the two hills, a fence blocked his way. Just as the thought registered that it would be impossible to get over the barrier, a cannonball blasted a hole and cleared the way.

Nearly 600 Americans fell as casualties that day, which was about 20 percent of the colonial forces that fought. The British army lost nearly half of its men, with 1,034 casualties. Ebenezar Herrick of Methuen died at the battle. Joseph Hibbard was wounded and died three days later. When word reached Methuen that James Ingalls was seriously wounded, his sister

Methuenites found themselves in the thick of the fight at the Battle of Bunker Hill. This photo shows a portion of the Bunker Hill diorama depicting the militia in battle. *Courtesy of the author.*

Dorcas rode to Cambridge on horseback to take care of him. Unfortunately, he died three weeks after the battle, on July 8.

Methuenites continued to serve during the American Revolution, taking part in many of the major battles identified in history books. But, it was these first two battles that set the stage for independence. A decision could have been made to accept the restrictive policies of the British government, but instead, these men and women chose to stand up to tyranny. Methuen historian Joseph Howe once wrote that they had a "universal, deep-seated determination[…]to protect their rights, at all hazards."

A simple marker, dedicated on June 17, 1907, at the corner of Pleasant and Pleasant View Streets today serves as a reminder of the choices these men made, and the risks they took, so that we may enjoy our freedom.

THE GREAT CHAIN

During the American Revolution, men, both young and old, came forward to fight for liberty. The British government had been systematically taking away the rights of the colonists. While many from Methuen went off to fight in scores of battles, one Methuenite, Joshua Swan, found a different way to fight. He used his skill as a blacksmith to create a chain that was used to block the British plans for control of the Hudson River Valley.

Joshua Swan was born in Methuen on March 12, 1755, and according to historian Ernest Mack, Swan was an apprentice bound to Peter Marston before the war started. Marston ran a blacksmith shop on what is now Howe Street, near the intersection with Pleasant Valley Street.

As an apprentice, Joshua was bound to Marston for seven years. During that time, he worked at the forge for just room and board. In exchange, Peter Marston was responsible for teaching Joshua the blacksmith trade.

When word reached Methuen that the British regulars were marching toward Concord, Marston released Joshua from his apprenticeship so he could join the Methuen militia's pursuit of the British army. In June 1775, Swan also stood with his fellow townsmen at the Battle of Bunker Hill.

Three weeks after the battle, George Washington met the survivors. In his pocket were orders to transform this group of local militia into a formal army. Joshua's enlistment was nearly up, but the twenty-year-old reenlisted in Washington's new Continental army.

The army quartermaster learned about Swan's blacksmithing skills and sent him to Fort Ticonderoga in New York to work as a farrier, shoeing horses for the Continental army.

In the winter of 1778, Joshua was called to work on a special project near West Point, New York. The British navy had been attacking settlements along the Hudson River Valley just north of New York City. If the British navy controlled the river valley, it posed a great threat to the northeastern colonies. Washington understood this and wrote to General Putnam, "The importance of the Hudson River in the present contest, and the necessity of defending it, are subjects which have been so frequently and fully discussed, and are so well understood, that it is unnecessary to enlarge upon them."

Earlier attempts to block the river with obstacles, fire ships and a chain all proved to be inadequate to the task. What was needed was a larger chain placed near a sharp bend in the river near West Point. Forts on the heights above the bend would add military support to the iron obstacle.

In early February, Joshua Swan and other blacksmiths were brought to the Sterling Iron Works, thirty miles from West Point, to begin work on what

This drawing of the Great Chain monument at West Point, New York, shows the type of chain that was used to cross the Hudson River.

some began calling the "Great Chain." Each link was about two feet long and about eleven inches wide, made out of two-and-a-half-inch-square iron bar stock. Each link weighed about 114 pounds. A total of 750 links were needed to cross the Hudson River near the West Point cliffs.

Creating the chain was no easy task. Iron had to be extracted from the ore, formed into bars on a huge, heavy-trip hammer and then shaped into links. The forges operated on a twenty-four-hour schedule, with Joshua Swan and his fellow blacksmiths working long hours to get the chain ready before the first thaw of the river.

On April 6, the partially completed chain was floated downriver on log rafts and put in place. For the next three weeks, this continued as more links were made available. On April 30, the last of the links were put in place and the chain was securely attached to the shore. Historian Lincoln Diamant wrote, "Within the severe limitations of the period, manufacture of the great chain in a matter of weeks was a triumph of early American mass production with interchangeable parts, a truly remarkable industrial achievement."

For the next five years, the British never chose to test the skill of these craftsmen. The strength and placement of the chain in the river, itself a symbol of defiance, discouraged any attempts by the British at continuing north on the river. This technological and strategic feat, accomplished by relatively few men in a short amount of time, gets only footnote coverage in the history books, but is a wonder nonetheless. Without firing a shot, Joshua Swan and his fellow blacksmiths had defeated the British plans for controlling the northeastern colonies.

LAFAYETTE'S VISIT

To early nineteenth-century Americans, the Marquis de Lafayette was a hero of epic proportions. As a volunteer officer in the Continental army, it is generally understood that he was instrumental in getting the French government to support the fledgling United States in its war for independence. Fifty years after the American colonies separated from Britain, the United States invited him back as a show of its appreciation. In the summer of 1825, Lafayette's tour brought him to Methuen, but left behind memories for generations to come.

In 1777, the twenty-year-old Lafayette had joined the Continental army as a general. He served without pay and provided for his troops out of his own pocket. He fought in most of the battles of the American Revolution and was with Washington at Yorktown when the British surrendered. In 1824, President Monroe invited the Marquis de Lafayette to visit the United States for the upcoming fiftieth anniversary of the Declaration of Independence. In August 1824, he began his tour, which eventually included all of the then twenty-four states in the Union.

One of the stops on this tour was at the scene of the first major battle of the American Revolution—Bunker Hill. Davis's Company of Methuen men had fought there and three died during this pivotal battle. Lafayette was there on June 17, 1825, to participate in the laying of the cornerstone of a new monument. Thousands of people attended the ceremony, many of them veterans of the war. It would not be surprising if some of those present at the event were from Methuen.

Four days later, Lafayette left Boston for a dinner in Concord, New Hampshire. Josiah Quincy, the mayor of Boston, described the procession carrying the general as "three open barouches, each drawn by four horses, those attached to the general's carriage being perfectly white animals of noble appearance."

The people of Methuen were not aware of Lafayette's visit until the last minute. With only a few hours' notice, townspeople from the outlying areas hurried to the center of town to catch a glimpse of the nobleman. The procession was expected to arrive from the south, through what is now Broadway, in the afternoon. One newspaper wrote, "Self-appointed sentinels from the ranks craned their necks in the direction of Andover, and now and then gave out a false alarm of the approach of the three barouches."

As the anticipated time approached, people began to see a cloud of dust a half a mile away in the direction of Andover. Reverend Oliphant of the First Church Congregational later wrote of the event:

At length a great cry went up. "There they come!" Sure enough, a cloud of dust could be plainly seen, half a mile away, with many signs of commotion in that direction. The girls put their hands to their back-hair, the men to their neckties and waistcoats, mothers gave a last touch to infant noses and forelocks, attitudes were struck, and resolutions were formed by more than one onlooker to be the finest figure upon which French eyes would rest that day. The dust and commotion grew nearer. The procession was advancing more rapidly than had been anticipated. Suddenly in a screaming panic, the crowd scampered in all directions to make way for—Major Osgood's bull! The animal had gained what Lafayette had fought for, liberty, and, not being a Christian, was using it "as an occasion for the flesh."

When Lafayette finally arrived, an enthusiastic crowd met him while a band of local musicians played martial music. After a few remarks from Lafayette about the cordial welcome he had received, the procession continued on to the New Hampshire border for a reception in that state's capital later that evening.

This small town was touched by the presence of this Revolutionary War hero. The opportunity to see such a public figure of international reputation would have been enough for a lifetime of memories, but the distraction of a love-struck bull seared this event in the townspeople's memories for generations to come.

Methuen Citizen Soldiers of '64

On April 12, 1861, Confederate artillery fired on Fort Sumter in the harbor of Charleston, South Carolina, forcing its surrender. The country was on the verge of collapse, and newly elected President Abraham Lincoln called for seventy-five thousand troops to protect the nation's capitol. Massachusetts answered the call, and over the course of the war, raised more than 150 regiments to preserve the Union. Methuen sent its share of men, with Company B, First Massachusetts Heavy Artillery, known originally as Methuen Light Infantry, serving nearly the entire war. Their experiences, first in Washington and then in the thick of battle, were some of the most unusual of the conflict.

Leverett Bradley of Methuen was the first captain of Company B, First Massachusetts Heavy Artillery. This company became known as the Methuen Company.

When the news of Fort Sumter's surrender reached Methuen, the selectmen in town asked Leverett Bradley to form a company of volunteers. Bradley, a farmer and shopkeeper from Methuen, had been prominent in the state militia at the Lawrence Armory and was perfect for the task. Enlistments were for three years, and he had no problems recruiting.

The Methuen Light Infantry was designated Company B of the Fourteenth Massachusetts Infantry by the commonwealth, and because of his recruiting efforts, Bradley was chosen the captain. On June 15, the more than one hundred men left Methuen for the forts around Washington, D.C. Before they left, though, the women of Lawrence gave Bradley a sword and other "equipments" and David Nevins donated material from his rebuilt Pemberton Mill in Lawrence for proper uniforms.

Garrison duty near Washington, D.C., was lonely and boring. Little comfort had been provided for the soldiers. One of the highlights, however, was during the spring of 1862, when Charles H. Tenney visited Company B in camp near Washington. He presented a revolver to Captain Leverett Bradley from the "Citizens of Methuen."

Eventually, camp life became more tolerable. Elaborate barracks were built, as was a dance hall. The regiment even sponsored a library for the soldiers. Because Company B was located first in line on the way from Washington, dignitaries visited them first and often. President Lincoln, Massachusetts Governor Andrew and Julia Ward Howe were some of the dignitaries who visited.

At some time in 1862, the regiment began training as artillerymen. Muskets were put aside and cannons were put in their place. From 1862 until the regiment was called into action in 1864, all training was focused on handling the cannons and mortars. In fact, the Fourteenth Regiment Massachusetts Volunteers were officially notified of the change on September 19, 1863. On that date, they were known as the First Massachusetts Heavy Artillery.

In March 1864, President Lincoln appointed General Ulysses Grant as head of the Army of the Potomac. Grant had a reputation as a fierce general who was willing to accept large numbers of casualties. This was something the South could not afford to do.

On Saturday morning, May 14, 1864, the soldiers of Company B, along with the rest of the regiment, were once again given muskets and told they were going to the front. These relatively green troops who had spent the last two years training as artillerymen were now told they would fight as infantry. Company B left for the front that evening. Three days later, after traveling by steamer and then marching twenty-three miles, Company B and the regiment arrived near a little town in southeast Virginia known as Spotsylvania Courthouse. Confederate General Ewell was making an attempt to capture the Union supply train and general headquarters. First Massachusetts Heavy Artillery was sent to stop him.

The company arrived about 1:00 a.m. and was met by the sobering site of long lines of ambulances bringing the wounded from the fighting nearby at the "Bloody Angle." At 6:00 a.m., the men were marched about a mile or more to form a line of battle supporting an artillery battery that was in action. They stayed there until 4:00 p.m. while rebel shells passed overhead. At noon on May 19, 1864, fighting could be heard in the distance and Company B, along with the rest of the regiment, moved two miles to a farm where rebel cavalry was spotted. One soldier wrote, "It was like a stroke of lightning from clear skies. In an instant the scene was transformed from peace and quiet to one of pain and horror." The Confederates attacked with savagery. The same soldier later wrote, "The cries of pain from loved comrades, wounded or dying; the rattle of musketry; the sound of leaden missiles tearing through the trees and the dull thud of bullets that reached their human marks produced a feeling of horror among those whose ears could hear." Fighting became intense. The Methuen company attacked the Confederates, hoping to push them out of the area. General Ewell's forces stopped attack after attack. Company B and the First Massachusetts Heavy Artillery were unable to push the Confederates back. Amid the carnage, Company B held its ground. Eventually, fresh Union troops joined the attack and by morning the Confederates were forced to withdraw.

The sergeants of Company B were photographed near the end of the war.

Soldiers were required to bury the dead after the May 19, 1864 battle near Harris Farm, Spotsylvania, Virginia. *Courtesy of the Library of Congress.*

On the fields of Harris's Farm lay the dead and dying of the battle, Confederate and Union alike. Losses to Company B from Methuen appeared to be the highest in the regiment. In this battle alone, fifteen men died. Nearly thirty-five men were wounded and eleven men later died in captivity at the infamous prison camp at Andersonville. When word reached Methuen about the losses, the community took it hard. The town sent representatives to Virginia to look after the wounded.

Company B continued to fight battles in places like Cold Harbor, Petersburg and Appomattox. In all, 325 Methuen men answered President Lincoln's call. This was more than was expected of the community. In defense of the Union, 52 of those lost their lives. For many more, their lives changed forever as a result of the war.

The commitment and sacrifice of these soldiers should serve as a reminder that freedom is a fragile thing, purchased with the blood of those who stand in defense of it. The unique experiences of these Methuen men stand today as a memorial to that commitment.

TWENTY-SIX ACRES OF HELL

To those who are aware, the words "Andersonville Prison" bring to mind images of unspeakable horror. Young men—Union soldiers, the best the country had to offer—living in squalor, reduced to skeletons and covered in rags no longer worthy of being called clothing. Among these unfortunate prisoners are a group of men who called Methuen home.

By 1864, the time when Methuen soldiers began showing up as prisoners of war, the numbers of prisoners captured by the South had progressed to such a point that they had become a burden on many Southern cities. The empty warehouses that served as prisoner-of-war camps had become inadequate to keep the prisoners from escaping. A new, remote area was selected to hold these men in Macon County, Georgia, near the small community of Andersonville.

Fort Sumter was the official name of the camp and it accepted its first prisoners in late February. Charles Varrell was the first prisoner from Methuen to be sent there, and what he witnessed as he entered the gates must have made his heart sink. The camp was originally built to hold ten thousand prisoners, but because General Grant had refused to continue the prisoner exchange with the Confederate army, the numbers quickly swelled to more in just weeks. By July, the prison camp held more than thirty-three thousand men on its sixteen and a half acres. This is more than the population of Salem, New Hampshire, living in an area slightly larger than the Grey Court Park. The camp had no shelters and the only water available was a freshwater stream that ran through the center of the camp. The stream served as a source of drinking water and as a latrine.

It wasn't long before Private Varrell had company from Methuen. After the Battle of Harris Farm outside of Spotsylvania on May 19, 1864, eight others soon joined him. Eventually, twelve soldiers from Methuen were held in the camp.

One Methuen native, Lucius Wilder, later wrote of his experience upon arriving: "The prison gates were swung open to receive us, and we saw the prisoners in rags, some of them with hardly clothing enough to cover their nakedness, some of them living skeletons." He described his feelings at this sight by writing, "It was enough to strike terror to the stoutest heart."

Photographer A.J. Riddle was able to capture this image of rations being issued to the Union prisoners at Andersonville on August 17, 1864. *Courtesy of the Andersonville National Historical Site.*

Within the walls, the soldiers lived as best they could. Scraps of wood, old blankets and uniform parts from dead prisoners were used to build crude shelters against the brutal Georgia summer sun. Those without shelter dug holes in the ground to try to get out of the hot summer sun. Rations were never sufficient. In fact, rations of meat were often left in the blazing sun for days before being given to the prisoners. It wasn't long before prisoners began dying under these conditions.

In August 1864, ten more acres were added to the camp, but it was too late for Methuen native Samuel F. Sawyer. The twenty-seven-year-old shoemaker was the first from Methuen to die at Andersonville, on August 2, 1864. He had joined the Fourteenth Regiment Massachusetts Infantry at the start of the war. His unit was later converted to the First Massachusetts Heavy Artillery and he was one of those captured at Spotsylvania, Virginia. The cause of death was listed as diarrhea, which was probably a result of drinking contaminated water. Malnutrition and disease were the leading causes of death in the camp. Frederick Emerson, a twenty-eight-year-old shoemaker, and William K. Messer, a twenty-nine-year-old farmer, also died from diarrhea. Albert Kimball, a twenty-one-year-old shoemaker, died of debilitas, which medical books describe as a wasting away. Henry Palmer, a twenty-three-year-old shoemaker, died of unknown causes. The last to die was James Gutterson, a thirty-nine-year-old butcher, of a painful vitamin deficiency called scurvy, at the end of September 1864.

James Gutterson's story was somewhat unusual. Lucius Wilder wrote that after he had been captured, he was hustled to the rear. "Jim Gutterson, of Company B, was terribly wounded through the body. I dressed his wounds

Prisoners were dying in such numbers that trenches were required to systematically bury the dead. This photo was taken on August 17, 1864. *Courtesy of the Andersonville National Historical Site.*

with bandages, which he carried in his pocket. We carried him about a half a mile and left him in an old house in a clearing. I supposed at the time that he was fatally wounded." Jim Gutterson had survived four months in camp, in some of the most unsanitary conditions imaginable, with such a terrible wound, only to die of scurvy.

For those who survived, life in the camp became hell on earth. Another former inmate, Private Sneden of New York wrote, "to hear the[…]shrieks, oaths and moans of the [dying] in their delirium was horrible." Methuen native Lucius Wilder agreed by writing in his memoirs, "The prisoners[…]were dying off very fast, 125 to 150 a day." According to Private Sneden, the corpses were piled up all day in the sun and taken out at sundown.

By the time the war ended and the camp was closed, over eleven thousand men had died. Most died a horrible death from disease and malnutrition. Of the twelve prisoners from Methuen, only four survived. The rest had lost their struggle to withstand some of the most inhumane conditions individuals have been forced to endure. For those that returned, they carried with them the memories of their ordeal, and the knowledge that their fallen comrades did not die in vain.

A Trust Betrayed

On Thursday, February 28, 1878, Charles Whittier told his wife he was going to Boston on some business. He was the town treasurer and collector, so it was not unusual for him to do this, and he had done so often. What was out of the ordinary was that by Saturday he had not returned. Instead, Whittier's wife received a letter from him stating that he had run off with all of the town's available funds. Thus began one of the most bizarre incidents in Methuen's history.

Charles Whittier was born in Methuen on April 25, 1828. According to the *Lawrence Daily Eagle*, Charles lived in Methuen until adulthood. His adventurous spirit soon had him traveling throughout the South. He first moved to Charleston, South Carolina, then to Providence, Rhode Island, and then eventually to New York City. While in New York, the South Carolina militia attacked the Federal fort in Charleston Harbor, sparking a long and bloody war.

This attack must have influenced Whittier's next move and his sense of adventure. In the fall of 1861, he joined a Massachusetts regiment commanded by General Butler of Lowell, and found himself in the mosquito-infested Mississippi River Delta.

Little is known about his time in the war, but it appears that it was short-lived. After his service, Whittier moved to Chicago and lived there a number of years. According to the *Essex Eagle Weekly*, he lost everything when the Great Chicago Fire took place in 1871. He eventually returned to Methuen.

Whittier quickly made a name for himself. He began purchasing tenement houses and increasing his wealth. The 1874 town records showed that he was elected one of the field drivers in town and was listed as a juror.

The following year, Charles Pelham, who served as town clerk, treasurer and collector, died and left a vacancy for those positions. Charles Whittier was elected to fill all three positions at a special town meeting.

For the next two years, Whittier was reelected to all three positions, and by all appearances, performed the tasks to the satisfaction of the town. During a routine audit of his accounts on February 1, 1878, everything appeared to be in order. The treasury showed a balance of $11,926.

In fact, all was not in order. For some time, Whittier had been using town funds for personal use. A year earlier, he had taken $2,500. The money was replaced before the town discovered the shortage. Where the money went was a mystery. The local newspapers wrote that, "[H]e had no extravagant habits[…]and employed no servants." The *Lawrence Daily Eagle* wrote, "He seldom went out of town, had no season tickets to Boston; and there appears to be no authority for the story that he lost the money in stocks." He may have just used the money as down payments for the many properties he purchased, with the expectation that the money could be returned before anyone found out.

As March 2, 1878, approached on the calendar, Whittier began to panic. The town accounts would need $8,000 to pay the teachers on that day. Whittier knew there was not enough money in the accounts to cover this, and he would finally be exposed. He started planning his escape.

He needed travel money, so he cashed a $500 check at the National Bank in Methuen, drawn on an account he had at the New England Trust Company in Boston. He then went to Boston and cashed another check. This time, it was for $800 from the same New England Trust Company account, leaving a $20 balance. When the Methuen bank check reached Boston, there was not enough in the account to cover it.

Whittier wrote to his wife from Boston, explaining what he was doing. To delay the delivery of the letter to his wife, Whittier put that letter in an envelope addressed to the postmaster in New York City, with instructions to forward the enclosed letter to his wife. He then left for Canada.

Whittier's wife received the letter on the day the money was owed the teachers. She immediately went to see Daniel W. Tenney with the letter. Tenney, along with three others, held the bond for Whittier, and if the money was not recovered, they were responsible for replacing it.

A meeting was immediately called with the selectmen, and they got the courts to issue an arrest warrant for Whittier. They also began looking into exactly how much money was missing.

The selectmen eventually determined that more money was missing than the original $8,000 that was due to the teachers. Tax money had been collected in February from many Methuen residents and that money was missing also. In the end, it was determined that Whittier had stolen the town's entire available funds, which totaled $12,500. There was no money left for town business.

Nearly two months went by with no word from Whittier, but on Thursday evening, April 19, 1878, two women traveling toward Lowell thought they saw a man who looked like Whittier. He was traveling on foot at about 11:00 p.m. They questioned what, exactly, they saw, so they waited until Friday morning to report it.

Police were sent to Whittier's home, where they found Charles Whittier, and he was taken into custody. The *Lawrence Daily Eagle* described Whittier as "in feeble condition suffering greatly in body in mind." When asked how he got home, Whittier explained that he had arrived in Boston late Thursday afternoon, had taken the last train to Lowell and walked from there. He said nothing else about what had happened and the police chose not to question him further there.

At the town meeting held that same day, "it was quite evident that the blood of the town was up," wrote the *Lawrence Daily Eagle*. The town was looking for restitution. The arraignment was held before a judge at Town Hall on Broadway and Whittier agreed to make restitution. It was believed that his properties could cover some of the cost and that wealthy relatives in Cambridge would help with the rest.

Exactly how much money was repaid, or if any additional punishments were given to Whittier, is not known. In order to create some closure, in 1882, the selectmen agreed to "omit from the next statement of the 'Financial condition of the town' the item 'Charles S. Whittier $7235.44' and all other accounts they may consider worthless."

The town had been a victim of an egregious act, but this peculiar incident ended as it began. The town had put too much trust in the honor of an individual, and that trust was betrayed each time.

THE PEAT MEADOW MURDERS

On a summer evening in 1908, a horrible event, known today to only a handful of people in the community, took place in the west end of Methuen. Special Officer Francis McDermott and Constable Charles H. Emerson, while on a routine assignment to investigate the theft of vegetables, were brutally murdered. After nearly one hundred years, the murders of these two men have never been solved. Their deaths became a sobering reminder of the risk that police officers must take in order to protect our community.

On the evening of August 8, 1908, Emerson and McDermott were sent to a section of the west end of Methuen known as "Peat Meadow" to investigate complaints of missing hay and vegetables from area farms.

Charles Emerson, a carpenter and builder by trade, was fifty-six years old. Married and a father of one daughter, he had lived in Methuen for more than forty years and had once served as the chief of the fire department. For the previous fifteen years, Emerson had been elected constable in Methuen. Frank McDermott was about fifty years old and married with two sons. For the previous twenty years, he had served as a special police officer. He once worked as an engineer at a local yarn mill.

Peat Meadow was an out-of-the-way section of land between what are now Elm Street and Forest Street. Constable Emerson was familiar with the area because he had been sent out there in the past to remove the hobos and tramps who frequented the area. There was an old slaughterhouse and shed in the woods that the tramps used for shelter, and it was believed that the culprits could be found there. The two officers left the station at about 10:00 p.m., and unless an arrest was made, the officers were to go to the Pleasant Valley section of town by 7:00 a.m.

When they had not reported in by 9:00 a.m., the police chief became concerned about their whereabouts. Calls were made to their homes, and when it was discovered they weren't there, the police initiated a search. Chief Jones and other officers checked the Pleasant Valley area first because it was thought that the missing officers might have just arrived there late. When they hadn't been found by 3:00 p.m., the police turned their focus on Peat Meadow.

After nearly an hour of searching, Police Chief Jones found Officer Frank McDermott's body in the bushes near a run-down shed. Nearby, on the other side of the shed, was the bloody body of Constable Charles Emerson. His skull had apparently been crushed.

The local newspaper featured the story on the front page for a week and a half. The state police was called in to help with the investigation and at one point the local state militia was also called in.

The murders of Special Officer Francis McDermott and Constable Charles H. Emerson had a chilling effect on the community. Residents were in a state of panic. Many refused to go out at night, fearing that the killers could strike again. Fueling this fear was the local newspaper. In a misguided attempt to find the murderers, all nonnative-born individuals were suspects. One headline stated that a Syrian family was being sought for questioning. Another covered the interrogation of a Polish boy. All of these leads proved to be fruitless, and were a sign of the suspicion people felt about new immigrants in the area.

Eventually, evidence started leading to a link to a previous murder in the Forest Hills section of Boston. Members of the Gutman gang of Jamaica Plain were suspected in that murder and a woman involved with

The bodies of Charles Emerson and Francis McDermott were found near this makeshift slaughterhouse. The white signs mark where the bodies were located. *Courtesy of the Methuen Historical Collection.*

the gang had sisters living on May Street in Lawrence. It was believed that members of the gang were hiding out in the area of the old Peat Meadow slaughterhouse. Police believed that the sisters were helping the fugitives with supplies of food. The theft of vegetables and hay may even have been the work of these fugitives.

On the evening of August 8, this information was not known to the officers. The police officers may have discovered the fugitives and thought they were only petty thieves. When the officers tried to arrest the fugitives, a fierce struggle took place near the shed. Others in the gang, hiding in the slaughterhouse and most likely attracted to the scuffle, went to help their partners. It was at this time that it is believed that the officers were shot. Charles Emerson was shot in the chest and Frank McDermott was shot in the leg, neck and then the head. McDermott apparently did not die quickly. Pools of blood were found in different spots in the area, indicating that he tried to continue to fight with his attackers. Investigators felt at the time that before Emerson and McDermott died, one of them severely injured one of the criminals. Before the fugitives left, the two officers were dragged into the bushes, and that may have when Emerson's skull was crushed. A massive multistate search was begun, and after months of searching for the killers, it appeared that they had escaped. The killers of Special Police Officer Francis McDermott and Constable Charles Emerson were never found.

These two men put their lives on the line to protect the community. They took the same risks that police officers today must face each day. We should remember their dedication and sacrifice, and be grateful to those who continue this tradition and wear the badge today.

THE SEARLES SWINDLE

Millionaire Edward Searles was a collector. Furniture, tapestries, architectural elements and even highly prized historical artifacts were part of his collection. It has been said that at one point, he had the finest collection of Guggenheim Bibles in the country. Always one to carefully check out the history of each piece he bought, it is a mystery that he, and the town, could be swindled over a piece of chain thought to be part of the 1778 Great Chain of West Point.

Edward Searles always had a taste for the finer things in life. As a boy, when most other children his age were working or going to school, he was learning to play piano and organ. He had a particular interest in designing home interiors, and later in life he chose that as his profession. As an employee of two prestigious interior design firms, he was witness to the opportunities that wealth provided.

Shortly after his marriage to Mary Sherwood Hopkins, widow of the wealthy Mark Hopkins of the Union Pacific Railroad, Searles began to indulge in his hobby of collecting antiques and historical artifacts. While abroad in Europe, he would select treasures to bring home to Methuen. Once they were home, elaborate rooms and buildings were designed to display the recently purchased treasures.

It is not surprising that, after Searles purchased sculptor Thomas Ball's Washington Monument, he wanted to embellish it with an appropriate historical artifact. The perfect piece was a section of chain said to be from George Washington's Great Chain of West Point. According to the seller, a salvage dealer named Francis Bannerman, sections from a historic chain were available for purchase. Bannerman claimed that this chain stretched across the Hudson River in 1778, blocking the British fleet.

Edward Searles purchased these chain links, believing that they were from the chain that crossed the Hudson River during the American Revolution. *Courtesy of the Methuen Historical Collection.*

Bannerman had acquired the chain when he bought out another salvager who had purchased it at a Brooklyn navy yard auction years earlier. According to historian Lincoln Diamant, Bannerman even published a pamphlet with what he purported to be an accurate history of the chain he was selling.

Wealthy collectors from all over contacted the junk dealer, a wealthy man himself, looking for a piece of American history. The Coast Guard Museum, the Chicago Historical Society and the Smithsonian all eventually acquired some of the links. The problem was that this chain did not have the history that Bannerman had assigned it. These links were from a later period and were manufactured in a Welsh iron mill near Cardiff, Wales. Historian Diamant quoted from a private memoir, "English iron manufacturer [Sir Lothian Bell] recognized [the chain] as one of the Admiralty buoy chains made by his firm, which had been used in New York harbor."

It is surprising that so many wealthy individuals and institutions were taken in by the hoax. Surviving historical links could be seen at the West Point Military Academy, and the original 1778 contract for the chain described the links as a very different size from those being offered. The contract said that each link was about two feet long and about eleven inches wide, made out of two-and-a-half-inch-square iron bar stock. Each link weighed about 114 pounds. Bannerman's links weighed nearly three times that. If that wasn't enough to put into question the authenticity of the chain, manufacturing techniques should have removed all doubt. Bannerman's chain was made of rolled steel, with beveled edges. This type of steel did not come into existence until 1844, more than sixty years after the historic chain was supposed to have been manufactured.

Despite all of this, Searles bought thirteen links from Bannerman sometime between 1900 and 1913, and placed them behind the Washington Monument on Lawrence Street. Each link was to represent one of the original thirteen colonies. A letter from Francis Bannerman to a person requesting more information about the links suggested that Searles bought the last thirteen links.

The false impression continued for many years as townspeople looked upon the chain with a sense of pride. It was their physical connection to an important event in American history. According to local historian Ernest Mack, in 1958, when the statue was sold to Forest Lawn cemetery in California, a group of history-conscious townspeople quietly cut one of the links from the chain so that this connection to the past would not be lost to the community. It was given to the Methuen Historical Commission. Seven links eventually made it to California. The other five were kept by Searles's heir, Benjamin Rowland, for his Vermont home.

For most of the twentieth century, the community held onto the belief that its link was an important historical artifact. But by the 1980s, the hoax had been discovered. This link of chain, so proudly displayed as a connection to the past, was a fraud. It was nothing more than discarded iron, past its useful prime as a mooring chain. Searles, who had been so careful to determine the authenticity of the things he collected, fell victim to a skilled con artist offering the illusion of a precious link to the past.

INFLUENZA EPIDEMIC

Influenza is a disease that has affected just about everyone more than once during a single lifetime. Deaths are rare, but when they occur, it is to the most vulnerable of the population—the very old, very young and those with weakened immune systems.

In the fall of 1918, a deadly strain of the flu invaded Methuen, killing not only the weak but the strong as well. No one was safe. For nearly six months, the community was paralyzed with fear and helplessness as the disease struck not only Methuen, but also the rest of the world.

The deadly strain of influenza, known at the time as the "Spanish Flu," was first reported in Boston at the end of August, when sailors began complaining about their health. An earlier strain had been found in Kansas in the spring, but by fall the virus had mutated into the deadly Spanish Flu. Within a week, Boston was treating over three hundred people and reporting its first deaths.

The virus quickly spread to other communities. By mid-September, nearby Lawrence recognized the threat of the disease after two deaths, and began discussing ways to stop the spread.

The first recorded death in Methuen was on September 25, 1918, when housewife and mother Margaret Ripley, age thirty-three, died at home. Within the week, nine more from Methuen died of the disease and its related pneumonia. An earlier death of a three-year-old on September 12 may have been from the flu, but was recorded as bronchopneumonia.

This was no ordinary virus. Symptoms began with a general weakness and severe aches. Fevers quickly rose to nearly 105 degrees. A third-year medical student wrote, "As the lungs filled[…]the patient became short of breath and increasingly cyanotic [blue in color]. After gasping for several hours they become delirious and incontinent, and many died struggling to clear their airways of a blood-tinged froth that sometimes gushed from their nose and mouth."

As the death toll increased, the Methuen Board of Health began taking action. Schools were closed, as was the library, and at the suggestion of the Massachusetts Board of Health, churches and clubs were asked not to meet until the worst was over. Milkmen were told not to enter homes when delivering milk because of the threat of catching the disease. Placards were placed on all houses where influenza was present to warn the public to stay away.

The disease continued to spread. Public officials, police officers, firefighters and even doctors and nurses became ill with the disease.

Throughout this time, the board of health tried to reassure the public that things were under control, despite increasing numbers of victims. On October 4, it was reported in a *Methuen Transcript* article that there were 162 documented cases of influenza in Methuen. Just that week, 28 new cases were reported. In the same article, the reporter wrote, "It is believed that now the authorities have the situation well in hand." This report was made at the same time that the board of health chairman was himself suffering with the disease.

The magnitude of the disease became overwhelming for the only hospital in the area, Lawrence General. The need for a temporary hospital for the more serious cases became apparent. State and federal officials advised that a regional hospital be established because of the shortage of medical staff. The state guard medical officer was called in to oversee the new hospital. The Lawrence Armory building was chosen, but then it was rejected because of unsafe conditions in the building. A tent hospital was established on Emory Hill in Lawrence and Ward G was set aside for Methuen patients.

The *Evening Tribune* reported, "Undertakers were on the base hospital grounds day and night, waiting for persons to succumb to the ravages of the disease[…]One tent where a patient was dying was found four undertaker's cards tacked up with their telephone numbers listed."

The base hospital on Emory Hill was off-limits to everyone except medical personnel and volunteers. Family members were kept informed of the condition of their loved ones by reports received twice a day from a messenger sent for that purpose.

When the disease entered a household, it often swept through the entire family, leaving them devastated in its wake. The Dumont family of 20 Piedmont Street lost three of their four children in one week. It is unimaginable the horror and despair they must have felt as each child suffered the ravages of the disease. Their feeling of hopelessness must have been enormous as they and their fourth child began showing symptoms.

Another problem quickly arose as parents became sick or occupied with tending to other family members suffering from the illness. Children were not being cared for properly. Some went without food for long periods of time.

This new crisis was brought to the attention of the board of health. Soup kitchens were established for those who could remain home. For those parents unable to take care of their children, a temporary children's hospital was set up in a portion of the All Saints' Church (now St. Andrew's) on Messer Avenue.

By the end of March 1919, the Spanish Flu had run its course. Variations of the disease returned in the fall of 1919 and in 1920, but not with the same destructive power seen in the 1918 strain.

In the end, it was estimated that over eight hundred people in Methuen were stricken with the disease and more than eighty-five died. It was the single most devastating disease to hit Methuen in such a short time. For six months, daily life ceased as the community united to fight one of the greatest threats to the people of Methuen.

TERROR ON THE TROLLEY LINES

A loud explosion shattered the morning calm in the eastern part of Methuen. A trolley car traveling to Haverhill struck a bomb buried under the tracks on Jackson Street, destroying the trolley's undercarriage. Though no one was killed in the explosion, this cruel act of terrorism on May 8, 1919, exposed Methuen to the increasingly violent labor disputes of nearby Lawrence.

For nearly three months, Lawrence textile workers had been on strike. They sought a forty-eight-hour workweek, an eight-hour workday and increased pay for overtime. Unfortunately for them, the high demand for textiles had dropped after the war, and mill owners were reluctant to give in. By May, tensions were running high, and threats of violence were reported daily in the local newspapers.

It was in the early morning hours of Thursday, May 8, 1919, when someone buried two dynamite-packed tomato cans on the trolley tracks near Brook Street in Methuen. At about 6:00 a.m., the first streetcar of the day, carrying about seventy passengers, passed over the bomb, which detonated under the trolley. According to the *Evening Tribune*, "The explosion lifted the car and threw the passengers about in great confusion." Windows on the right side of the trolley were blown out into the street. Fortunately for those in the trolley, no one was hurt. The trolley had a steel undercarriage that absorbed most of the blast. When the police examined the scene, they found the other unexploded can and another unexploded stick of dynamite.

The police were told that there had been some suspicious activity in the area that might have been connected to the bombing. They discovered that a short time before, dynamite had been stolen from a nearby farm. Wires had been cut near the explosion scene and an axe head had been found wedged in the switch at the nearby track siding.

Three days after the first explosion, the bombers struck again. This time it was on Merrimack Street in Lawrence. Three bombs went off under a trolley, frightening the passengers and causing considerable damage; again, no one was injured. Police were on heightened alert but no suspects could be found.

It was becoming apparent to the police that nonstriking millworkers were the target, and these acts of violence were designed to terrorize and intimidate these workers. Police were desperate to find the criminals before they struck again; exactly one week after the first explosion, a third attack took place.

This time, the bomb was placed on the tracks on Haverhill Street near Glen Forest. When a trolley struck the bomb at 1:00 a.m. on May 15, 1919, it lifted off the tracks as windows were blown out. Five feet of track were also destroyed in the blast. Luckily, the car was empty of passengers, but this attack claimed its first injury—motorman Harry Greenwood suffered slight injuries on his thigh.

Three and a half hours later, Methuen police got a break in the case. A two-pound bomb was found buried under the tracks at the corner of East and Gloucester Streets. For the first time, a disaster was prevented.

For nearly a week, the investigation continued, but no new clues were found. Fortunately, attempted attacks had stopped while labor leaders negotiated an end to the strike. Then, on May 22, 1919, a settlement was reached and workers returned to their jobs. Though investigations continued, the bombings ended and no one was ever held accountable.

These attacks had caused nearly three weeks of fear and anxiety in the community. They stopped as abruptly as they began, ending the nightmare but offering no resolutions or clues to the identities of the perpetrators.

KILLED IN THE LINE OF DUTY

Sometime about 1:00 a.m. on the morning of August 1, 1923, the Methuen Police Department received a call about an attempted burglary in the west end of town. Someone, the caller reported, was trying to break into a camp on the Merrimack River, near the Roseland Ballroom. Officers Arthur Bower and John McDonald were sent to investigate. Within the hour, this seemingly routine call would leave one officer lying in the street mortally wounded and the other beginning one of the strangest unsolved investigations in Methuen police history.

Officer Bower, a five-year veteran of the police department, and his partner, the relatively new man John McDonald, left the police station shortly after the call. According to newspaper accounts, when they arrived near the Roseland Ballroom on Lowell Boulevard, they saw two cars parked on the side of the street some distance apart. Bower and McDonald approached the first car and noticed three men inside. Not forgetting the second car, Bower told his partner to take the patrol car and check out the second vehicle. When Officer McDonald left his partner, he saw him standing on the running board talking to the three men inside.

According to an August 3, 1923 *Methuen Transcript* article, "When McDonald pulled down the road he turned and was surprised to see the other car in motion toward Lowell, with Bower on the running board. Shots were fired and Bower rolled to the road."

At least eight shots, from two different guns, were fired at Officer Bower. One of them struck Bower in the abdomen, hitting his spine. Another hit him in the leg while he was lying in the road. Bower was able to get off all six shots from his gun before the suspects got away.

Officer McDonald immediately began chasing the fleeing car, firing his gun as he drove. As the car disappeared in the darkness, McDonald returned to his stricken partner and found him "lying wounded and writhing in great pain."

Neighbors had heard the shots and came running to the area. They helped get Bower into the police car and McDonald drove his partner to Lawrence General Hospital. According to local newspapers, Bower died a short time later while in the operating room.

An investigation began immediately. Officer McDonald said that when they approached the vehicle, they noticed that it was a green Paige touring car with New Hampshire plates. McDonald couldn't remember the whole number on the plate, but he did remember it started with "44." Bower and McDonald got a good look at two of the occupants because Bower had shined a flashlight into the car. One strange fact that McDonald told other investigators was that he didn't hear the shots even though neighbors, blocks away, said they heard about fifteen shots.

Lowell police were notified, as were Manchester and Nashua Police Departments. All cars matching the description given by McDonald entering these cities were stopped and inspected. As the hours ticked away, it appeared that the criminals had gotten away.

Theories surfaced almost immediately as to who the criminals were. The most popular idea floated was that they were rumrunners afraid of being caught with illegal liquor.

One suspect was soon identified when a taxi company owner reported that one of his cabdrivers was missing and suspected of stealing a taxicab. The cabdriver, Barney Banks, had last been seen near the Roseland

Ballroom earlier in the evening. The next day, he was picked up in Hartford, Connecticut, and brought to Lawrence for questioning.

At first, the investigators thought they had the case wrapped up. Banks confessed to being involved in the murder and implicated a young Cornell University veterinarian student, who was training in Methuen, as an accomplice. An elaborate story was told and he even gave a detailed account of the shooting. He told the police that they had five quarts of liquor in the back and were afraid they would be discovered.

The police noticed some inconsistencies and when Banks was confronted about them, he changed his story. The veterinary student was cleared.

Over the course of the next ten days, Banks told five different stories about Officer Bower's murder. In the process, he had named six different people as accomplices. These even included his fiancée and an army buddy. Each story was investigated and each proved false. Time was being wasted chasing down false leads.

Banks was very convincing, but as time went on, the police and the public began to question his sanity. One newspaper said, "Banks is of the mentality which baffles observers. He may either be possessed of a shrewd, criminal cunning, or may be of the befuddled, stunted, impressionable type, who, under the strain of hours of questioning might inexplicably associate certain facts that he read with his own personality."

A doctor was eventually called in to examine Banks. After observing the suspect for some time, the doctor felt that the self-proclaimed killer was not the person the police were seeking. The doctor found that Banks was a pathological liar. Barney Banks's imaginative fantasies squandered precious investigative time, leaving this case unsolved and a mystery that remains to this day.

A Christmas Tragedy

For those who celebrate Christmas, it can be a time of joy. For the Kilmurray family of Methuen and the Barker family of Salem, New Hampshire, there was much to look forward to in the coming year of 1929. Instead, a tragic event on Christmas Eve 1928 changed their lives forever.

John Kilmurray must have believed that his life was blessed. By 1928, he had been working for three years as the personal chauffeur of Harriet Nevins, the widow of industrialist David Nevins. Driving her to various appointments exposed Mr. Kilmurray to a world he would never have experienced in his home city of Pawtucket, Rhode Island.

Kilmurray was a handsome, well-dressed man. The twinkle in his eye and his quick smile put anyone he met promptly at ease.

Kilmurray lived with his wife Mona and two daughters in a saltbox-style house behind the Nevins home on Hampshire Street. Nearby was the garage that housed Harriet Nevins's automobiles. When not driving Mrs. Nevins to appointments, he would be found either in the garage tending to the cars or playing with his daughters.

According to his oldest daughter, named Mona like her mother, Kilmurray was a clever man, but a bit of a prankster. In an interview, Mona said that her father would like to take his daughter skating on a pond behind the house in winter. On one occasion, instead of ice skates, her dad put roller skates on the three-year-old. The wide base of the wheels helped her stand up on the ice. In another instance, Mona said her dad put her in a tree with Mrs. Nevins's German shepherds, Vora and Max, and took a photo of her eating dog biscuits with the dogs.

Frank Barker, on the other hand, was a quiet man. He worked as a carpenter at the Arlington Mills on the Methuen–Lawrence line. He lived

John Kilmurray found it humorous to put his daughter, Mona Kilmurray, in a tree with Harriet Nevins's dogs. *Courtesy of Robin Stolarz.*

with his wife Emma and three children, ages one to seven, in Salem, New Hampshire, near the Salem depot.

On Christmas Eve 1928, the thirty-seven-year-old John Kilmurray was asked to deliver some Christmas presents to some of Mrs. Nevins's friends and acquaintances. One of the stops was on Broadway near the Nevins Library. Shortly after seven in the evening, Kilmurray drove north on Broadway and parked the car. As he was removing some Christmas presents from the trunk, another car driven by Frank Barker slammed into Kilmurray, pinning him between the two vehicles. Kilmurray was rushed to Lawrence General Hospital in serious condition. Both legs had been crushed and he had lost a lot of blood.

A call went out to the residents of Methuen and Lawrence for blood donations. Methuen's police chief, Frank Seiferth, was one of three donors. Kilmurray's right leg was so badly damaged that the doctors were concerned that gangrene would set in if they didn't amputate it. At 1:00 a.m. on Christmas morning, the doctors removed Kilmurray's right leg. John lingered between life and death for nearly two days, but early in the morning of December 27, John Kilmurray died.

Frank Barker had been arrested at the scene of the accident, but with the death of Kilmurray, new charges were filed. This time he was charged with manslaughter.

The accident had a devastating effect on both families involved. Kilmurray's wife now had the responsibility of raising two very young children on her own. For a time, Mrs. Nevins helped out. Mona and her daughters were allowed to stay in the chauffeur's cottage. They eventually found another place in Methuen to live. Mona never remarried, so money was always tight. Mrs. Nevins helped by giving the family thirty-five dollars a month until the children were adults.

For the Barker family, the accident was never discussed. Barker was not known to abuse alcohol, so it was assumed that he had just been celebrating the holiday with some friends after work. The court revoked his driver's license and fined him for the accident.

The memory of the accident haunted Frank. According to his daughter Doris, he refused to drive until late in life. She said that the family never even owned a car. Relatives would drive him to work at the Arlington Mills. When the mills closed and he worked as an independent carpenter, clients had to drive him to and from the work site. It wasn't until his senior years that Frank started driving again. Even then, it was reluctantly and at his wife's urging.

Barker always felt responsible for Kilmurray's death and at one point even contacted the Kilmurrays to apologize.

Thirty-seven-year-old John Kilmurray was delivering Christmas presents for Harriet Nevins when he was struck by a drunk driver on Christmas Eve. *Courtesy of Robin Stolarz.*

Ironically, many years after the fatal accident, Frank Barker and his family became victims themselves of a drunk driver. Though this accident was not fatal, it did send some of the family to the hospital and was a reminder of the randomness of such a senseless tragedy.

Though this Christmas Eve accident in 1928 took place in the blink of an eye, the momentary lapse of judgment by one person had devastating effects that were deep and lasting. Mona and her sister lost the love of their father and the secure life that a father can provide. Frank Barker carried with him the guilt of causing this loss for the rest of his life.

About the Author

Dan has been involved in Methuen's historical organizations for more than thirty-five years and writes a monthly Methuen history article for *MethuenLife* magazine. He has coauthored two books—*Images of America: Methuen, Massachusetts* and *Bunker Hill: Battle, Monument, Memory*—and has served as president of the Methuen Historical Society, chairman of the Methuen Historical Commission and as a founding member of the Merrimack Valley Preservation Group. Dan is married to Diane Gordon Gagnon and has two children, Jeff and Katie, and works as a park ranger for the National Park Service.

Visit us at
www.historypress.net